BLUEPRINTS
The Poetry Book

Moira Andrew and David Orme

Stanley Thornes (Publishers) Ltd

Do you receive *BLUEPRINTS* **NEWS**?

Blueprints is an expanding series of practical teacher's ideas books and photocopiable resources for use in primary schools. Books are available for separate infant and junior age ranges for every core and foundation subject, as well as for an ever widening range of other primary teaching needs. These include **Blueprints Primary English** books and **Blueprints Resource Banks**. **Blueprints** are carefully structured around the demands of National Curriculum in England and Wales, but are used successfully by schools and teachers in Scotland, Northern Ireland and elsewhere.

Blueprints provide :
- Total curriculum coverage
- Hundreds of practical ideas
- Books specifically for the age range you teach
- Flexible resources for the whole school or for individual teachers
- Excellent photocopiable sheets - ideal for assessment and children's work profiles
- Supreme value

Books may be bought by credit card over the telephone and information obtained on **(0242) 228888**. Alternatively, photocopy and return this **FREEPOST** form to receive **Blueprints News**, our regular update on all new and existing titles. You may also like to add the name of a friend who would be interested in being on the mailing list.

Please add my name to the **BLUEPRINTS NEWS** mailing list.

Mr/Mrs/Miss/Ms --

Home address --

---Postcode ------------------------

School address --

--- Postcode ------------------------

Please also send **BLUEPRINTS NEWS** to :

Mr/Mrs/Miss/Ms --

Address --

--- Postcode ------------------------

To: Marketing Services Dept., Stanley Thornes Ltd, FREEPOST (GR 782), Cheltenham, GL50 1BR

Text © Moira Andrew and David Orme 1995
Original line illustrations by Atelier Illustrations © ST(P) Ltd 1995; artwork on page 5 by Charlotte Firmin.
'June 21st – A day in the life of the sun' © Margaret Blount 1995, 'Water moods' © Gary Boswell 1995, 'On our side of the playground' © John Cotton 1995, 'In the kitchen' © John Cotton (previously published in *Two by Two*, John Cotton and Fred Sedgwick, Collins Educational), 'Sing a song of many wheels' © Maggie Holmes 1992 (previously published in *Pribble Prabble*, Sherbourne Publications), 'The sad bus' © Ian Mcmillan 1995, 'A tree has secrets' © Andrew Mines 1995, 'Sea song' © Tony Mitton 1993 (previously published in *Early Years Poems and Rhymes*, compiled by Jill Bennett, Scholastic), 'Glad to be alive' and 'Listen to machines' © Ian Souter 1995, 'The train is a dragon' © Jill Townsend 1995, 'The silver tree' © Dave Ward 1995. All other poems © Moira Andrew and David Orme.

First published in 1995 by:
Stanley Thornes (Publishers) Ltd
Ellenborough House
Wellington Street
CHELTENHAM GL50 1YD
England

A catalogue record for this book is available from the British Library.

ISBN 0–7487–1909–1

Typeset by Tech-Set, Gateshead, Tyne & Wear
Printed and bound in Great Britain

CONTENTS

INTRODUCTION

The *Poetry Book* is a carefully structured book offering a developmental approach to reading and writing poetry in primary schools. It contains detailed teacher's notes with a wide range of suggestions for use in the classroom, a number of anthology pages including collections of poetry for reading, performing and displaying, and a wide range of topic-based photocopiable copymasters for poetry writing. For infants and Key Stage 1 the topics covered are:

- 'Creatures'
- 'Day and night'
- 'Family'
- 'Feelings'
- 'Games'
- 'Numbers'
- 'Seasons'
- 'Wheels'
- 'Wind and storm'.

For juniors and Key Stage 2 the topics covered are:

- 'Elements'
- 'Mythical beasts'
- 'Portraits'
- 'The sea'
- 'Senses'
- 'Space'
- 'Trees'
- 'Wonderful world'
- 'Machines'.

Although the copymasters have been designed to support work throughout the primary school, the classification of the topics should not be seen as too rigid: many of the pages will work well across a wide age-range. In this way the copymasters can build confidence in the less able writer, yet still stretch the high flyers. We have offered a range of ways to present the work of children, such as display and performance. We would stress the importance of the speaking and listening element in poetry, not just in listening to and performing poems from the anthology sections and completed work by children, but in the writing process itself at the brainstorming and drafting stage. A collaborative approach, either in pairs with a response partner or in groups, is always valuable.

The topics selected are those particularly suited to poetry, with possibilities for direct observation and experience and an emotional response. The best poetry comes from looking closely at the world around us and exploring and talking about areas of immediate concern to children – their homes, their families and the environment in which they live, with all its colours, sounds, shapes, textures, feelings and emotions. The copymasters are intended to stimulate imaginative responses to the children's own lives rather than provide rigid, mechanical exercises. Although the focus is on language, many of these pages can add a personal, creative dimension to other areas in the curriculum such as science and technology.

In addition to the copymasters, each topic contains substantial **teacher's notes**, offering a range of suggestions for using the pages, ideas for follow-up work and display possibilities. Always refer to these notes before starting work on one of the copymasters, as we have deliberately kept the instructions on the copymasters themselves to the absolute minimum to allow plenty of space for the child's own writing.

The **anthology pages** contained in each topic build up into a substantial collection of poetry for reading, performing and display, and for providing inspiration and models for new writing. Many of the poems have been specially written for this book. Teachers should supplement them with a wide range of poetry for children to listen to – longer poems, narrative poems and a range of pre-twentieth century poetry. The anthology poems themselves can be blanked off when photocopying, providing an attractive range of frames for displaying the children's work.

At the beginning of the book we have provided a major resource bank of ideas and suggestions, including:

- Starter ideas
- Guidance on the writing process – finding ideas, brainstorming, drafting, proofreading
- Guidance on poetry patterns, vocabulary-building and making images
- Guidance on display, publishing, bookmaking and performance
- Guidance on assessing children's writing
- Ideas for a poetry week in your school.

A **skills index** shows the coverage of both poetic and language skills, and enables the teacher to take several informed routes through the material on offer.

HOW TO USE THIS BOOK

Children should always be encouraged to see writing as a process, not as something that is done all in one go. This is the philosophy that runs throughout these materials.

The Poetry Book is intended as a highly flexible resource. The teacher can, of course, use the various sections as a whole to add an extra dimension to a class topic on, say, numbers or the environment, and the subjects are broad enough to make them relevant to a number of different starting points. Alternatively, the teacher can mix and match pages for other purposes. If listening is a concern, for example, the **skills chart** can be used to find a range of different approaches to listening skills. Techniques described in one topic – haiku in 'The sea' for example – can be slotted into another topic or used as part of a scheme of work looking at different poetry patterns. Copymasters can be used on a one-off basis as a useful 'end-on' activity for children who have completed a task, or for extension work for able children.

Using the copymasters

Poetry should not, of course, be about endless worksheets. However, the copymasters can perform a useful part of the teacher's poetry work by providing:

- A starter or stimulus
- A framework for writing, particularly useful for those children less confident in handling language
- A model for children's own writing
- An attractive display end-product
- Ideas for the teacher to adapt in ways appropriate to his or her needs.

In some instances, the final piece of work should be written in the space on the copy of the copymaster. This should not be done until the poem has been worked on in draft, and checked for accuracy.

Other photocopiable pages

On page 9 there is a **photocopiable drafting checklist**. This can be reduced to allow children to stick it into their drafting books, or enlarged to make a wall poster.

The **'spidergram' brainstorming diagram** on page 4 can usefully be copied and used to start a piece of writing.

STARTERS AND STRUCTURES

The diagram below shows the process of writing and what activities are relevant at each stage. The solid lines represent the movement from one stage to the next; the dashed lines indicate that assessment is an on-going process, applicable to all stages.

The following notes work through all the stages except for 'Presentation', which is covered in a separate section on pages 10–13.

The process of writing

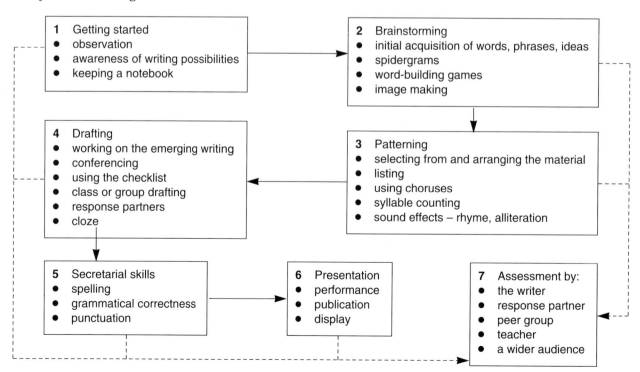

1 Getting started
- observation
- awareness of writing possibilities
- keeping a notebook

2 Brainstorming
- initial acquisition of words, phrases, ideas
- spidergrams
- word-building games
- image making

4 Drafting
- working on the emerging writing
- conferencing
- using the checklist
- class or group drafting
- response partners
- cloze

3 Patterning
- selecting from and arranging the material
- listing
- using choruses
- syllable counting
- sound effects – rhyme, alliteration

5 Secretarial skills
- spelling
- grammatical correctness
- punctuation

6 Presentation
- performance
- publication
- display

7 Assessment by:
- the writer
- response partner
- peer group
- teacher
- a wider audience

Getting started
A problem for writers of all ages is finding ideas! *The Poetry Book* provides many stimuli that help to solve this problem, but the children will want to be able to write poems based on their own observations and experiences, using the models or forms provided by the copymasters rather than the material itself.

Observation
An important task of the teacher is to sensitise children to the writing possibilities in their own lives. Real experiences – physical and emotional – make the best poetry. Sometimes these experiences can be 'created' by the teacher, by bringing interesting objects into the classroom for example, or by taking children out of the school to look first hand at the weather, living things, and urban and rural landscapes. The art of the poet is to make humdrum experience special:

I saw
A red bus groaning and grumbling
Down the street,
And in my imagination it became
A tired old dragon,
Puffing out smoke
Because its fire had gone out.
'Watch out' it said.
'I may be old,
But I can still
Swallow you up!'

Try a 'poem hunt' with your class. The children should be taken out, notebook at the ready, with instructions to record all the things they see that might start a poem. A poem hunt from an urban school might end up like this:

Date 2nd May
Time 10.00 a.m.
Place Market Street, Cheltenham

litter bin – too full –
rubbish tipping out

noisy traffic – green buses – fumes

traffic warden –
black and yellow
like a wasp

man on wobbly bike
dirty pavements

rubbish in gutters

lorry blocking road – warning flashers –
unloading washing machines

ambulance siren screaming

shops – treasure caves
supermarket
letter boxes
shoe shops
green grocers
Woolworths
book shop

bank
money machines
eat plastic
give you money

people –
hurry dawdle chatter
push babies in pushchairs

puddles like mirrors

street signs

zebra crossing – green man
beeping noise

In the park – old people in the sun – sitting on damp benches

Poetry notebook

Children used to this exercise will have included observations, words, phrases and tiny images, all of which might be 'seeds' that will turn into poetry. Back at school, children need to select the ideas that are most interesting and brainstorm them, either with other children or by themselves, without worrying about spelling and presentation. This is easier for them if they understand the writing process and know that spelling and presentation are important but come at a later stage.

Brainstorming
There are many ways to go about the process of brainstorming. Whichever is chosen, however, the process should not simply be random but should be structured.

Brainstorming is a skill that needs to be demonstrated. We recommend that, at first, the whole activity from brainstorming through to the completed poem should be undertaken as a class activity, using the board or OHP. Once the class have gained confidence, they can undertake the activity themselves, using the brainstorming model you have provided. It is also valuable to start off a brainstorm on the board or OHP with just a few ideas carefully selected from what is offered, and then to ask the class, in groups, pairs or individually, to complete it before they start their first draft. They can then use a few of the ideas in the class brainstorm to add to new ideas of their own.

Providing a framework
One possible framework is to provide headings. Over the page is a brainstorm on the theme of shopping.

3

Action	Description	What you saw	What you heard / felt / smelt
push ⎫ trundle ⎬ trolley	colourful bright friendly hungry greedily expensive	tins - frozen food bread, cakes, meat fruit and vegetables food from all over the world toddlers being a nuisance bright colours everywhere	checkout - dinging - bleeping - clattering smell of bread cooking - makes you hungry - makes you spend more money! packets of peas - freezing cold!
goods are - stacked - piled - heaped			
customers - stretch - bend - shout - pay			

Word pictures

tins - metal mountains. freezers - north pole, shoppers dipping like polar bears. checkout sounds like out of tune orchestra. checkout person - a mugger taking all your money.

Other ideas

What about people with no money? - Hungry faces looking through the window. Shoppers looking forward to getting home.

Shopping brainstorm

The **spidergram** (shown below) is a popular way into brainstorming. This enables ideas to branch out from a central concept.

There are other possibilities, but the key objective is that children have material from which they can build their poem. No child should be given a blank piece of paper and be asked to write a poem on it.

Always encourage older children to have a pencil and paper when a class brainstorming session is in progress, and insist that they put their ideas down on paper before putting their hand up. All teachers will know the blank face of children who have forgotten what they were going to say!

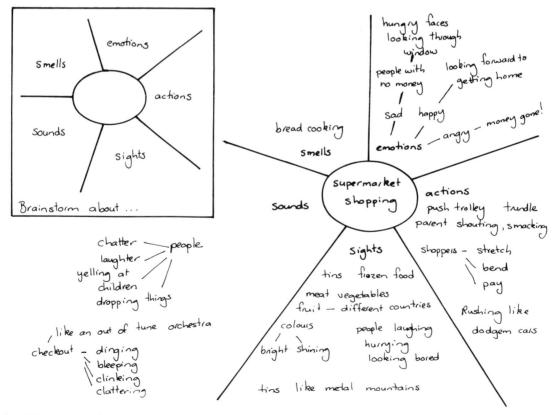

A blank spidergram model and a completed shopping spidergram

Brainstorming with younger children

Working with younger children and with less confident writers requires a different approach. The list or brainstorm needs to be built up with a question and answer session, either with an individual child in a conference, or with a group or the whole class. This can include an element of storytelling, as in the example below, where the teacher acts as scribe. The children will relate anecdotes of their own experiences when shopping, while the teacher is filtering, encouraging, setting targets ('let's think of five things') and generally guiding the process in a structured way.

Here are some typical questions asked by the teacher to develop a shopping brainstorm with a group of Key Stage 1 children:

Who helps with the shopping?
Who pushes the trolley when you go shopping?
What sorts of food can you buy? Let's think of five things. (The teacher is looking for categories – e.g. vegetables, tins, frozen food, meat – rather than specific items.)
What can you hear and smell in a supermarket?
What makes Mum and Dad cross?
What funny things have happened to you in a supermarket?

Turnabout poems

Brainstorm ideas on one subject, then use the vocabulary and images to write about something else. For example, a brainstorm about volcanoes will produce some interesting and lively language for a poem about school, with the volcano idea as an extended metaphor and/or simile:

Mr Brown was cross!
His rage erupted in assembly,
And his words rained down on the children
Like hot lava …

Word-building games

Word-building games are of great value in building vocabulary and in developing confidence in handling language. They can be used as part of a brainstorming activity.

1   *Ordering words*
Children are asked to supply words on a given topic – this is a useful exercise for introducing the thesaurus. Here is a response to a request for rain words:

spitting
pouring
showering
cats and dogs
coming down in buckets
dripping
drizzling.

The task is to put the words in ascending order of bad weather. The words can then be used as the basis for a story poem in which the rain is getting heavier and heavier. Stories such as this are excellent for turning into picture books (see below).

Page from a book-writing project carried out at Southbourne Infant School, West Sussex

5

This exercise can also be done with abstract ideas:

annoyed
cross
angry
furious
in a rage.

A story could be written in which someone gets increasingly angry. Another alternative is to personify emotions:

I am anger.
I have red eyes and a staring face;
My nose is wrinkled and my teeth are showing.
I always speak very loudly,
And can bite when you are not expecting it!

A poem like this can form the notice on the side of a zoo cage, with children drawing the creature inside as shown below.

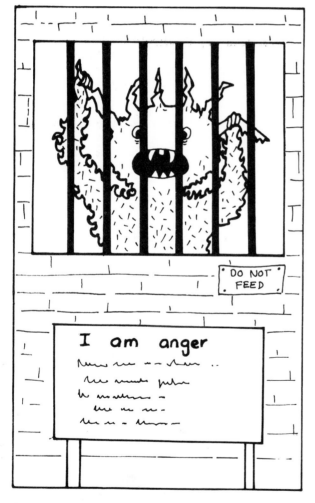

2 *Kennings*

Kennings describe something in as many ways as possible but using just one word. There is more information on kennings on page 71.

3 *Word list*

This exercise uses a list of given words which are combined at random, perhaps using dice, or by free choice. The words must be included in the poem, or even in the first line, changing the part of speech if required.

The word list below is a practical resource, a word bank to be copied and used in the classroom:

Namers	Doers	Describers
drum	drum	still
swallow	swallow	bright
leaf	clutch	ghostly
field	hide	scorched
flame	plunge	fat
cut	cut	cut
spider	rang	grey
axe	sing	furious
rock	gleam	gigantic
fingers	struggle	pale
mirror	squeeze	loudly
journey	sleep	wasted
peak	ride	whispering
star	clatter	slyly
flower	crawl	old
jar	sweep	glaring
ruin	lumber	deep
bone	tip	mysterious
gold	wave	bitter
machine	roar	wickedly
wind	stamp	vast
feather	whisper	stolen
time	crack	sharp
stream	hang	fair
mist	bend	dry
iron	slither	raw
clock	crumble	oily
shock	scrape	fresh
eye	freeze	angrily
scale	echo	soft
forest	pity	broken

Below is an example of a poem created from this list:

The forest echoed
to the singing of furious axes.

4 *Sound games*

This involves searching for and using words with a sound link – alliteration, rhyme or rhythm pattern. Start very simply with alliterative rhymes:

One woeful walrus wobbled in the wet,
Two tough tigers, tootled tiny tunes.

With older children, talk about how to reflect real sounds in poems, as in 'Beach music' (page 105) and in some of the work on machines and wheels. Children are usually poor at rhyming, but occasionally they can be helped to think in rhyme, even when the rhymes are excruciating. Start by making up lists of rhyme words – the *Penguin Rhyming Dictionary* is a useful resource for junior classrooms – and build the poem around these.

Patterning

Poems are words made into patterns. The patterns may be very structured and formal, such as the sonnet, or very informal with simply a sound link to give the pattern. An apparently totally unstructured poem still has a pattern – the poet has had to make the decision where to end each line and begin a new one. This is not a random process!

As soon as the brainstorming is over, the decision has to be made about what pattern the poem will take. Sometimes the pattern drives the poem, as in the simple acrostic (page 15).

Simple patterns for younger children
1 *Ideas + chorus*
This is the sort of poem that can be built up by a teacher transcribing the ideas of very young children.

>   Tins of beans stacked up high,
>   Bright red carrots waiting for a customer.

>   How much shall we spend today?
>   TEN POUNDS!

>   Lovely hot bread, smells delicious!
>   Frozen food, cold as snow.

>   How much shall we spend today?
>   TWENTY POUNDS!

2 *Question and answer*

>   What are we going to do today?
>   We're going shopping!
>   What are we going to buy today?
>   Tins of beans, to eat on toast,
>   Bright red crunchy carrots,
>   Lovely hot bread, delicious!
>   Frozen food, cold as snow.
>   How much will we spend today
>   Fifty pounds or more!
>   How will we feel today?
>   BROKE!

Patterns for older children
1 *Sound poems*
These can be alliterative and/or produced on an alphabetical or number basis, as in 'One woeful walrus' on page 6.

2 *Rhyme*
Rhyming is a difficult skill for children to master. However, they do enjoy rhyme and it is a shame to outlaw it. One way round this for younger children is to use a rhyming chorus only, while the rest of the poem doesn't rhyme:

>   This is what we'll buy today,
>   How I wonder will we pay?

An alternative is to 'borrow' an existing rhyme. For a rain poem for infants, use such traditional rhymes as:

>   Rain, rain, go away,
>   come again another day

or

>   It's raining, it's pouring,
>   The Old Man is snoring!

as a chorus.

There are a range of rhyming activities in this book. Stress that rhyme is good for story or funny poems but less good for descriptive ones.

3 *Word images*
Building word pictures through simile and metaphor is important in developing imaginative thinking.

a) Mini-poems
These offer a simple pattern – first line real world, second line the image.

>   Tea towels on a washing line;
>   White birds fighting the storm.

b) Stretching images
This uses a simple starter pattern:

>   The (real world)
>   Is a (image)
>   It (narrative)

For example:

>   The tea towel on the washing line
>   Is a white bird fighting the storm;
>   It flaps its wings,
>   struggles to reach the sky,
>   but cannot leave the ground.

For plural things the pattern can be changed to:

>   The
>   are
>   they

For example:

>   The goldfish in the pond
>   Are pound coins in a wishing well.
>   They sparkle in the sun,
>   And tempt me as if I
>   Were a hungry cat!

4 *Haiku*
The Japanese haiku (5–7–5 syllables) is good for tiny images based on sudden moments of observation and insight. There is more on haiku on page 101.

Syllable patterns require discipline in their production, and fighting with the form is a valuable activity. A more challenging pattern than the haiku is the **cinquain** (2–4–6–8–2 syllables). See the work on this on page 122.

5 *Poems that speak to objects*
Ask pupils to make a list of questions they would like to ask an object. They should select the best questions, then use them in a poem.

>   Tea towel on the washing line,
>   why do you struggle to escape?

This can lead to a reply.

>   I want to fly like a white bird,
>   right across the world,
>   but my foot was pegged down
>   by my cruel owner …

An alternative is a poem in which the object speaks directly:

> I am just a white tea towel,
> But if only I can get free …

Speaking to an object is just one of a range of poems in which the second person (you) is used directly or indirectly. Other possibilities are instruction poems, curse poems and odes (see below).

6 *Instruction poems (such as spells)*

> Take a pint of Octopus juice,
> Add some fur from a donkey's ear …

7 *Curse poems*
These can be fun but need handling with care.

> I hate you!
> May your hair fall out
> And your ears turn green …

8 *Odes*
In an ode, a person, object or abstract idea is addressed.

> O wild west wind, thou breath of Autumn's
> being …
>
> (Shelley)

9 *Poems that tell stories*
Brainstorm with a storytelling session. Suggest the sort of incident that can become a funny story – getting locked out of the house, breaking something, Dad burning the dinner. This can lead to short narrative poems or to story writing. Get children to work in pairs. It is a good idea to ask one child to scribe or use a cassette recorder in the first instance, while the other child ad-libs a story orally.

Drafting

Drafting is the process by which the brainstorm ideas turn into the final poem. Many teachers are concerned that this can be a time-consuming business, involving much head-to-head work between teacher and child. However, below we suggest a range of alternative drafting techniques, all valuable in getting to grips with the drafting process.

Drafting checklist
We suggest that the checklist on page 9 be enlarged to produce a wall poster, or copied onto a sheet that can be stuck inside the child's drafting book. Do not insist that the child works systematically through the list. Its purpose is to stimulate the writing process, not regiment it.

Class drafting
Drafting skills should be shown by the teacher working on the board, perhaps with a class poem or an unfinished poem by 'anon'. It is probably best not to launch into a poem by a child in the class. The technique is question and answer – the drafting checklist suggests the sort of questions the teacher might ask the class.

Group and pair drafting
Drafting is an essential part of the writing process and children need to see it as such, not merely as a demand to write their poem out again. Discussion is a valuable aid to writing and does not need to be just between teacher and pupil. Once children are used to the process they can work together constructively, either by drafting a group or pair poem or by reacting to a poem written by a partner.

Cloze
Use cloze procedure or sequencing as a basis for looking closely at a poem and for discussion on choice of words. The cloze exercise can concentrate on one particular part of speech – verbs, for example:

> They _____ the dogs and _____ the cats,
> And _____ the babies in the cradles,
> And _____ the cheeses out of the vats,
> And _____ licked the soup from the cooks' own
>   ladles,
> _____ open the kegs of salted sprats,
> _____ nests inside men's Sunday hats …
>
> (From *The Pied Piper of Hamelin* by Robert Browning)

This particular exercise can be fun if you change the pests from rats to a quite different creature – Martians, for example! Another possibility is to cut out the imagery, and look for good substitutes.

Line endings
In a non-rhyming, 'free verse' poem, children (and adult writers) are often unsure when to end a line and start a new one. The important skill to teach is listening – reading a poem aloud is the best way of finding out where the pauses or changes in the flow of thought occur. Try giving the class a poem reproduced in one long line, and asking them to cut it up with a pair of scissors. Insist that they read the poem aloud first.

Finishing poems
Weak endings are often a problem for young writers. Give the class a poem with a missing last line and ask them to come up with an interesting way of concluding the poem. Discuss the various options.

Secretarial skills

Many aspects that have a direct bearing on the meaning or structure of the poem will be worked out at the drafting stage. Grammatical confusions should show up as the poem is revised as well as punctuation which is a vital part of the 'music' of the poem. Secretarial skills such as spelling need to be tackled at a later proofreading stage.

Most junior children, especially in the early stages, will have a spelling book to write in new words as they encounter them. The problem with this is that it encourages children to drop the work already in progress in order to seek out the correct spelling. The children may well have forgotten why they wanted the word by the time they get back to their writing! Do encourage underlining 'best guesses' at spelling, then asking for help at this final stage. It is a hard lesson for children to learn as they see spelling as something

Drafting checklist

1 Are you happy with your poem? What did you want to say? Have you managed to say it?

2 Have you used a special pattern, and have you got it right?

3 Are you pleased with the words you chose? Think again about any you are unhappy with. Do you need all of the words? Cross out any that you don't need.

4 Have you read the poem aloud to someone? Are there any bits that didn't sound right?

5 Does your poem have a good ending?

6 Have you used interesting word pictures and comparisons?

7 Have you thought about punctuation?

8 Have you rhymed your poem? Does this make it better?

9 Have you checked your spelling? Get help if you need it.

10 What are you going to do with your poem now?

concrete that they can get right. If the class are aware of the writing process as outlined here this will help. Avoid unqualified statements such as 'spelling doesn't matter'.

Assessment

Many teachers find the assessment of children's writing problematic. This is quite understandable: the assessment of writing by adults is a fraught process and there is no reason why the work of children should be easier to make value judgements about.

Any numeric marking or grading of a poem is doomed to failure, simply because there are no fully satisfactory objective criteria to set it against. The best

poetry surprises with its unexpectedness, and the 'tingle factor' should not be downplayed. The drafting checklist (on page 9) can help with assessment; teachers may also find the list below useful.

- Does the poem look at familiar things in a surprising, new way?
- Has the writer made the best and most appropriate choice of language?
- Does every word count?
- How do the class feel about the poem?
- How does the writer feel about the poem?
- Did you feel a 'tingle'?

PRESENTATION

The final stage in the writing process is the presentation of the poem to an audience. This presentation may take the form of:

- Performance
- Publishing
- Bookmaking
- Display.

Children should be encouraged to see that writing has a public outcome. While much of the language work done in school is for a practical purpose – skill practice, record-keeping and so on – creative writing is intended for an audience.

Performance

A performance may be for other members of the class, for another class or for the school in assembly. Poetry may form part of a special presentation for parents. Whoever the audience may be, the work in preparing a performance is enjoyable and of enormous value in developing speaking and listening skills.

There are far too many dull poetry presentations where children stand up in turn to read out a piece of work. Often this is garbled or inaudible. This approach throws away all the opportunities offered by performance and should not be encouraged!

Some performance basics
Reading aloud is an art and one that deserves time spent upon it. Children need to be encouraged:

- To know the poem as well as possible. If they can, they should learn it by heart, even if they have the copy with them for security. The children need to look at the audience while they speak; they cannot do this if their head is in the poem.
- To think about pacing. Very often the sheer terror of performing in public leads to an undignified gabble, with the child rushing off stage as the last line is being spoken! Some of the group presentation activities can help with this, as can the use of percussion instruments to give pacing and rhythm.
- To think about expression, both facial and vocal, and in the use of the hands. Encourage children to

rehearse with a trusted partner who can coach and encourage.

Using movement and mime
An audience needs to be given something to do with their eyes while listening to the poetry, but they should not be distracted from listening by too much activity. One of the best means of achieving this is to do a movement activity between each poem. This works best if a group of children are involved in reading a sequence of poems. Possibilities are infinite. The following ideas are tried and tested, but the imagination of teacher and pupils will come up with many more.

- Start the children off in a circle, kneeling. The reader faces the audience and reads the poem. A drum rolls or tambourine shakes, and the circle moves round one place. The previous reader kneels and the new reader stands up and reads a poem. This continues until each child has read.
- Readers stand in two ranks, as shown below. Child A reads. A drum bangs, the first rank steps backward two steps and the rear rank steps forward two steps. Child B reads. A drum bangs again, and the process repeats with child C reading. This continues until all the children have read.

       B   D   F   H   J

       A   C   E   G   I

- Children form the pattern of the poem. If they are performing a series of haiku, for example, they stand as shown below:

▢	▢	▢	▢	▢			(5)
▢	▢	▢	▢	▢	▢	▢	(7)
▢	▢	▢	▢	▢			(5)

The children can read chorally, perhaps rearranging themselves between each poem.

The same idea can be used for cinquains, which will require 22 children – one for each syllable!

Pair reading
Children enjoy the security of working with a partner, but this is only one of the benefits; many poems lend

themselves to a reading by two people. Question and answer poems obviously work well, but so do poems involving a real world/imaginary world comparison, for example:

A   A tea towel on a washing line.
B   A white bird trying to fly in a storm.

Pairs will often start by reading lines alternately, but try and encourage children to be more imaginative than this. Some lines – choruses for example – might be read by both the children together.

The whole range of theatrical devices can be used in a poetry performance – costume, face painting, lighting, mime, music and images projected on an overhead projector. The possibilities are only limited by the stamina of the teacher!

Publishing

With the sophisticated technology now available in primary schools there is every opportunity for producing professional-looking booklets and anthologies that give contributors a real sense of pride. There are benefits other than strictly educational ones – school public relations, the opportunities for fund raising, etc. – but teachers should not lose sight of the educational value of such projects, particularly if children are involved at every stage, including the editorial ones.

Wherever possible, every child should have work included in a publication or display. Non-writers or children with special needs who are struggling with language may be represented by a poem transcribed by another pupil or special-needs assistant or by a poem written with someone else, in which they provided some of the ideas.

The spelling should be corrected in every case, as should grammar and punctuation unless there is a justifiable reason why not. If asked, children would want their work to be correct and they deserve that final input by the teacher. Obviously with very young children there is room for negotiation and too zealous a rewrite should be avoided. Involve children at the editorial stage. If it is necessary to veto a particular item, explain why.

Typesetting and layout

In general, photocopied handwriting is not attractive and the poems are better if they are typed up. Where possible involve the children, but this is a slow process for most and the teacher will probably participate quite heavily. If the publication is for a specific event leave plenty of time. Desk-top publishing systems in school provide a range of fonts and frames and enable pages to be laid out on screen. This is a valuable experience for children, who should be involved in the work even if the final result is not as restrained and tasteful as the teacher may wish!

Illustrations

A photocopied end-product allows a range of artwork to be included. Line drawings photocopy best, but scraper-boards and linocuts can also be very attractive. If offset printing is to be used for a special job the results can be quite spectacular.

Formats

A4 is the standard paper size in school, but this is not always attractive if produced as a booklet stapled down one edge. A5 (folded A4) or A4 from folded A3, stapled on the spine, looks better, but thought needs to be given to the layout stage to ensure the page order works correctly. The cover can be produced on card or coloured paper. An alternative to a booklet is a poetry newspaper, a single sheet of folded A3 printed on both sides.

Binding

Stapling is the obvious form of binding, and children can be very useful in collating pages. Booklets stapled on the spine require long-arm staplers. Spiral binding is an attractive alternative to stapling.

Bookmaking

The production of books gives enormous satisfaction to children, involves a wide range of practical skills and preserves work in a permanent form. The simplest strategy is to mount poems and illustrations in a 'big book' made of pieces of sugar paper sewn together on the spine. The poems can be handwritten or word-processed, and an attractive cover can be designed and perhaps laminated.

There are many other possibilities for original bookmaking:

● Produce your 'big book' in concertina form so that it can be opened out for display. Note that only one side of the paper can be used.

A concertina book

● Produce your book in a shape appropriate to the topic – tree-shaped, house-shaped and so on. A pond-shaped book can have a transparent cover (use an OHP transparency) and contain poems about pond creatures.
● Make picture books out of narrative poems, with just a few lines on each page. This idea can be the basis for interesting work on writing for an audience, with junior children researching picture books and writing their own for infant classes.
● Encourage individual children and small groups to produce their own books. These can be very simple, or imaginatively elaborate.

Display

Colourful and imaginative displays of work are an integral part of life in every primary school, and good display is as important to children's poetry as the written work itself. When arranged with obvious care, display demonstrates to the children that their work is valued by the adults in their world. There are many imaginative ways of displaying poetry, from the one-poem book to the large class frieze. The teacher's notes on the individual topics in this book describe in detail a range of appropriate display ideas, while here we provide an overview and some alternative suggestions.

● For a class frieze a child's work should be individually mounted, usually on matching backing paper, before being placed on the frieze. Pin the finished frieze at the eye level of the intended audience.
● Work should be cut to size on a safe trimmer and single or double mounted as funds and time permit. Pin up blocks of finished work so that the top and sides are level. Children often enjoy illustrating the borders of their poems with felt-tip pens or coloured pencils.
● Keep the poetry blocks to a single theme, for example springtime. Add drapes in related colours, poem cards, paintings and photographs. On a table beneath the display arrange books (anthologies and information books), plants and artefacts which can extend the scope of the chosen scheme.
● Try mounting the frieze with a cross-curricular theme, for example shape poems alongside maths work on geometrical shapes.
● Try and make the display involve the person looking at it. One possibility is to place the poems behind doors that have to be opened for the poems to be read. Another is to display inside-looking-out poems behind an opening window. Use the idea of different weather: feeling warm and comfortable inside, looking at the cold/wet weather outside. Try a display with four windows, one for each season.
● Display poems as mobiles. Poems can be shaped and displayed hung from the ceiling. This takes up no wall space. Mobiles are particularly suitable to describe things that can float or fly, or the sun, moon, stars and clouds. Write and decorate each side of the mobile so that the poems can be read as they turn in the breeze.
● Framed poems make an interesting display. Write portrait poems to describe classmates, teachers, historical figures and so on. Design a pen and ink frame in which to hang the pen-portraits. Poems about deep forests/snow-clad mountains/underwater can be set in an illustrated frame (trees, rocks, coral, fish, etc.) cut from a separate piece of card or paper.
● Poems written inside a lidded box delight even the most sophisticated children. Look at a small decorated box with the children. Talk about the mysteries it could contain if it were a magic box or held a secret. Write a poem called 'Box of dreams', 'Box of wishes' or 'Memories'. Cut out circles of paper and write the poem on the round. Design a 'lid' and staple it over the poem so that the reader has to lift the lid to read it.
● Banner poems can be displayed to great effect, not only in the school hall or corridor, but outside, hanging from or between trees. Write them for special occasions.

Staple the poems to drapes or crêpe paper and hang them above the front door to welcome parents and friends to the school. Spring or summer poems can be hung outside, when the weather is fine. Suspend the banners from the trees so they move in the breeze.
● Make a poetry tree. Cut out a large tree shape and let children write poems on leaf or flower shapes. Glue the flower/leaf/butterfly poems onto the poetry tree. A valentine tree is another possibility. Write poems on heart shapes and hang them from a valentine tree in the school hall. If these poems are anonymous it adds to the fun!
● Write and display the longest poem in the world. In groups, write a story poem on the chain-of-consequences principle, each section ending with the words 'and then'. Keep the poetry writing going over a few days and display round the classroom, along the corridor and into the hall.

Good displays should mark the children out as authors. They should encourage children and adults alike to stop and look, to read and appreciate the poetry they see. Children's poetry is usually interesting, often full of fun and occasionally a window into the soul. It is up to us to make it as inviting and accessible as possible. Good quality display does just that.

Poetry events

Many schools run book weeks – why not have a poetry week for a change?

● Invite a poet to your school. Many poets are experienced in working with primary-age children and can offer a range of performances and workshops. In the UK, contact addresses can be obtained from your local Regional Arts Board or from the Poetry Society (write to the Education Officer, the Poetry Society, 22 Betterton Street, London WC2H 9BU). Local libraries and school library services can be very helpful. Of course, visiting poets will charge fees and expenses but if funds are available a visit makes a very special highlight to a poetry week. A subsidy may be available from your Regional Arts Board – discuss with them the possibilities of more extended visits and residencies.
● Collect together as many poetry anthologies as you can muster. Contact school library services for help with this.
● Make poetry displays for the entrance hall. Use books and poetry posters. Mix children's work with that of the professionals.
● Leave a display area blank in each room in which a workshop is to be held so that work can be displayed and mounted at the end of the day.
● Have a number of writing reference books handy for writing sessions – dictionary, thesaurus and rhyming dictionary.
● Read favourite poems onto a tape recorder. Leave the book open beside the tape so that children can both listen and read.
● Think of ways of using poetry across the curriculum, for example in maths or science.
● Ask for favourite childhood poems from teachers and other adults in the school. Make a display of remembered poems and, if possible, old books.

- Run competitions. These do not have to set one poem against another – the competitive element could concern performance, display or illustration.
- Organise a bookshop. Tell your book supplier of your poetry focus.
- Involve parents and the community wherever possible.

- If funds permit, invite an artist or calligrapher into the school to work with the children.
- Dressing up as a poetry character can be a tiresome business for teachers. A simpler suggestion is to make hats that illustrate a favourite poem. These can then be presented in a 'hat parade'.

SKILLS INDEX ▶

Skills	Copymasters	Skills	Copymasters
Bookmaking	1, 18, 23, 37, 42, 68	Listening	5, 13, 29, 32, 34–5, 41, 48, 49, 51, 55, 63, 70
Brainstorming and word-building	2, 5, 7–9, 13, 18–20, 22, 24, 26–7, 31, 34–5, 38–9, 42, 47, 49, 54–7, 59–60, 62, 64, 66–69	Observing	8, 16, 35, 39, 49, 53–4, 56, 61, 65
Display	5, 7–9, 14–16, 18–21, 23, 27–8, 30, 33, 35–6, 39–40, 43–6, 54, 57, 59, 61, 64, 68–9	Patterning	3–6, 9–15, 18, 20, 22, 25, 29, 31–2, 36–8, 41–3, 45–50, 52, 54, 57–8, 61, 63, 65–6, 68
Drafting	1–72		
		Speaking/performing	3, 5, 10–12, 13, 15, 17, 19, 25, 32, 34, 48, 51, 55, 58, 63, 70
Image-making	1, 8, 26–7, 33–4, 38–9, 42, 50, 52–3, 57, 59, 62		

CREATURES

Animals are always a good subject for writing. Children have a natural affinity with them and all have some knowledge about their lives – homes, food, movement and so on. Creatures can offer colour, danger, action and a whole range of emotional links ranging from fear to love.

Use themes such as Noah's Ark, animals in danger, pets, farm animals, animals of the rainforest and so on. These days, circuses and zoos make less acceptable topics.

Copymaster 1 (Animal riddles)

A Animals, from tigers to creepy-crawlies, are ideal for riddles, as they are familiar to the children and each has some distinctive attributes. A good riddle, besides giving the opportunity for using image in a very direct way, should be something of a puzzle for the reader.

On the copymaster the top left-hand box demonstrates the principle of the riddle by turning the animal into a non-animal idea. Use brainstorming questions like 'Why "silver armour"?' 'What was the poet describing?' 'How else might one describe scales?' In the top right-hand box the children have to work out what kind of creature wears 'a bright red coat with black buttons', then draw the ladybird. For the bottom left-hand box the children must make up a riddle to describe an elephant – What does the baggy skin look like? What colour is it? What about the trunk? – and for the final box, the children draw and write an original riddle about a different creature.

Younger children will need some help to grasp the concept of a riddle. Talk about 'animals' in the classroom – if the blackboard/computer/chair was an animal, what sort of animal would it be?

Make the finished riddle into a one-poem book. Use a square of sugar paper or a sheet of unlined A4 and fold it as shown opposite. Write the riddle on the left-hand side and cut a flap on the right-hand side to hide the answer, which should be written underneath.

B Encourage the children to write animal stories, putting each new idea on a fresh line so that it looks like a poem.

> I am a tiger.
> On hot days, I sleep in the sun.
> But when I am hungry,
> I …

Make the animal story poems into a zigzag book. Use sugar paper, concertina-folded into the number of pages required. Illustrate each page with felt-tip or coloured pen.

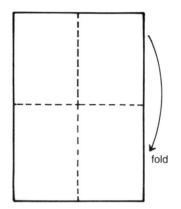

fold

cut

Making an animal-riddle book

Copymaster 2 (Snake words)

A This is a vocabulary-building exercise. Collect a 'shopping list' of words to describe the snake: its shape, pattern and movement. Encourage the children to think of snake images – like a rope, hose, lasso or lightning – making the exercise into a brainstorming session. Add these ideas to the word list on the copymaster.

Now put the words together into a shape poem inside the snake on the copymaster. Outline the snake in colour and give it a pattern. Join up the children's snake poems to make a long class poem or mount the individual poems on card and hang them from the ceiling. Make a jungle environment using tissue or crêpe paper and hang the snake poems among creepers and leaves.

B Make one-poem animal books shaped like the animal: a tall book for a giraffe, a fat book for a hippo, a stripy book for a tiger, a mini-book for a ladybird and so on (see examples over the page).

One-poem animal books

Copymaster 3 (A zoo in your bedroom)

A This works well as a class poem, perhaps for eventual performance. It follows the pattern of ideas/chorus, ideas/chorus, with a countdown element that is very popular with infant children. The animals should get bigger as the numbers become smaller – the children almost always end up with one elephant in their bedroom!

Each pupil should write his or her name on the copymaster to personalise the poem. Then they choose the animals and decide what they are doing to complete the poem. For younger children, build the poem as a class activity before asking them to build a poem on their own.

A chorus element always encourages performance. The class can perform the chorus, with individuals or groups taking the parts of the various animals. A variation is to have eight children for the eight ants, seven for the seven mice and so on. This requires 36 children in total. Make appropriate masks (see below) and add animal noises for dramatic effect!

B Try alliterative counting poems based on creatures:

Ten tame tigers twitching their tails,
Nine naughty nannygoats nibbling nuts,
Eight enormous elephants enjoying Easter eggs,
…

C Make up a poem similar to the one on the copymaster but this time with the animals running the school! Encourage children to think of ideas to suit different animals, such as:

A giraffe to fetch things down from high cupboards
An elephant to hoover the floor after lunch
A wise owl to be the headteacher
A woodpecker to …

Work on a short rhyming chorus like:

It's really great, it's really cool!
The animals have come to (your) School!

Copymaster 4 (Animal acrostics)
Acrostics, although familiar, provide a more difficult task than at first appears. On this copymaster the children have to complete the fish acrostic. There is also space for the children to develop their own animal acrostic at the bottom of the copymaster. Encourage the children to look for words and phrases that describe the animal in the poem, rather than simply choose random words to fit the down-line spelling out of context. The acrostic below tries to describe characteristics of the giraffe and is also an animal riddle.

What am I?

Good and tall to reach
Into the topmost branches and
Rip off the highest leaves
And the tastiest buds.
Far too tall to bend down for
Food fallen on the ground.
Exceptionally useful as a ladder!

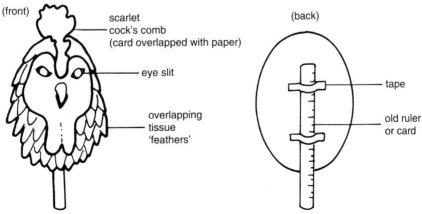

How to make a cockerel mask

15

Great and small

I'm a yo-yo
On a green string.
What am I?

I'm Mr Big Ears
With a tail for a nose.
What am I?

I sound like just one letter
But I'll fill your jar with sweetness.
What am I?

David Orme

Answers: Snail on a piece of grass, elephant, bee.

Cows in close-up

Cows are such lumbering creatures,
it comes as a great surprise
to see their long silky lashes,
their tender intelligent eyes.

They are such everyday creatures,
using tails to brush away flies,
giving us all that creamy white milk,
so gentle – in spite of their size.

They are such picture book creatures,
that it's hard to realise,
misty breath rising like smoke in the air
they're not *dragons* in disguise!

Moira Andrew

Animal riddles

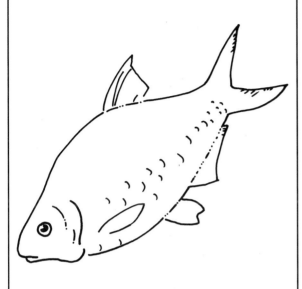

I'm an underwater knight
In silver armour.
Catch me if you can!

Even though I'm tiny
I'm easy to see
With my bright red coat
And black buttons.

Copymaster 1

Snake words

Can you think of more snake words?
Use some of them in your snake poem.
Write the poem on the snake!

coil

scales

hiss

tongue

flicker

slither

rope

_____

_____

_____

_____

_____

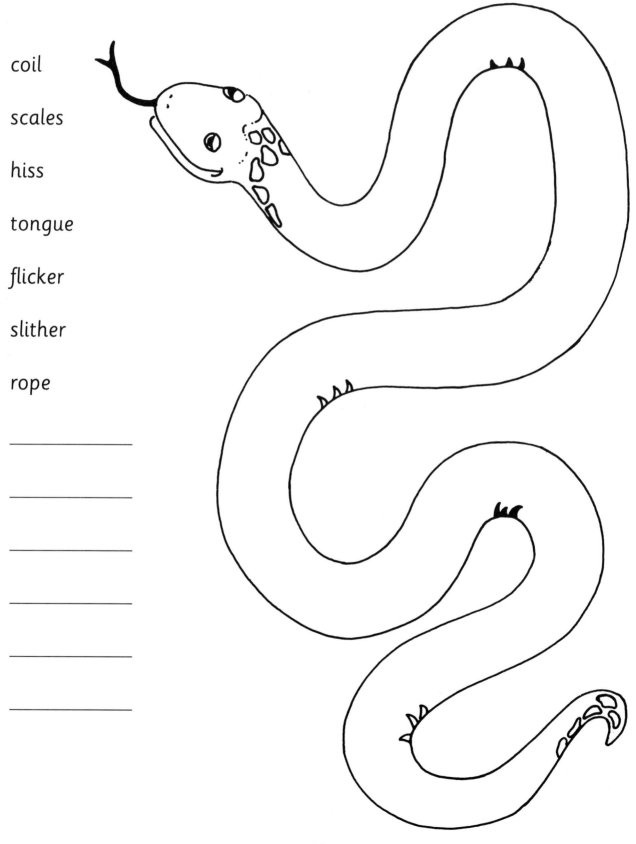

Copymaster 2

A zoo in your bedroom

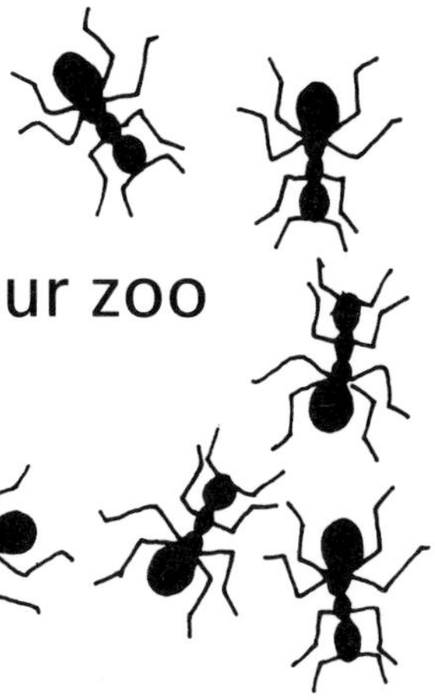

Write your name in all the boxes.
Can you think of some other animals for your zoo bedroom? What are they doing?

[_____]'s Bedroom

In [_____]'s bedroom there were:

Eight ants in a jam jar
Seven mice eating cornflakes

Six kittens _____

Five _____

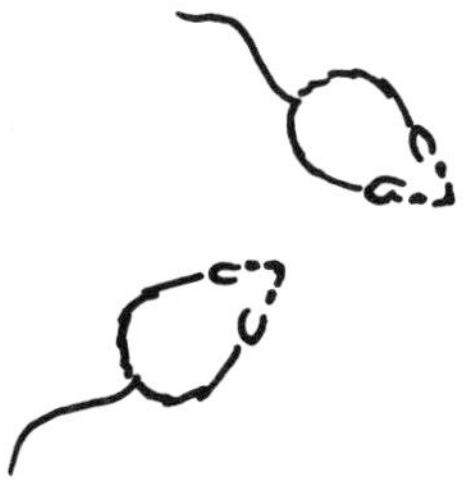

What shall we do?
What shall we do?
[_____]'s bedroom
Has turned into a zoo!

Four monkeys _____

Three _____

Two _____

One _____

What shall we do?
What shall we do?
[_____]'s bedroom
Has turned into a zoo!

Copymaster 3

Animal acrostics

Take care!
If I
Growl, it means I will
Eat you
Right up!

F _____

I _____

S _____

H _____

Curled up fast,
Asleep. DON'T
TOUCH!

_____

_____

_____

Copymaster 4

DAY AND NIGHT

Copymaster 5 (Things that go BUMP in the night!)
Sometimes when children are alone at night, with no light, no television and nobody to talk to, they feel frightened. Shadows become ghosts or bats or other scary creatures of the imagination. Talk with the children about their night-time fears and suggest that the best thing to do with such horrors is to make fun of them.

Get the children to work with a partner imagining all the things that might go BUMP in the night. Imagine seeing the wardrobe on the move, hearing the wind moaning, feeling the breath of dragons.

Ask them to list all the things that frighten them. Put them together to write a funny poem that rhymes. Encourage them to make it quite silly.

Read Moira Andrew's poem 'Who's afraid of the dark?' on page 23. Children can borrow the line 'I'm not afraid of the dark, not me!' to put at the end of each verse of their own poems. A model for the first verse is included on the copymaster.

Display the completed copymaster as a window poem. Cut out the poem, glue it in the middle of a sheet of black paper and on a top sheet make a border of ghosts, skeletons and so on. Cut out an opening window with patterned curtains. Open it to show the poem (see below).

Copymaster 6 (Clock poem)
This is a poem that works well as a performance piece and is an obvious aid for learning to tell the time. The times inserted in the poem do not need to be whole hours. 'It's half past two' or 'It's hometime' will give a variety of rhythm. In each case the clock hands should be drawn. Display the finished poem on a cut-out grandfather clock background.

Copymaster 7 (Day and night)
[A] This copymaster builds up the vocabulary of day and night words, making it into a mini-thesaurus. Children, individually or in groups, extend the lists by brainstorming. The words can be used in a poem of contrasts, perhaps alternating day and night ideas. Day poems can be written in black on white paper, night poems in white or coloured pencil on black or purple paper. For example:

A town street

In the day, cars rush and roar
Down our busy street.

At night, a lonely cat
Patrols the dustbins.

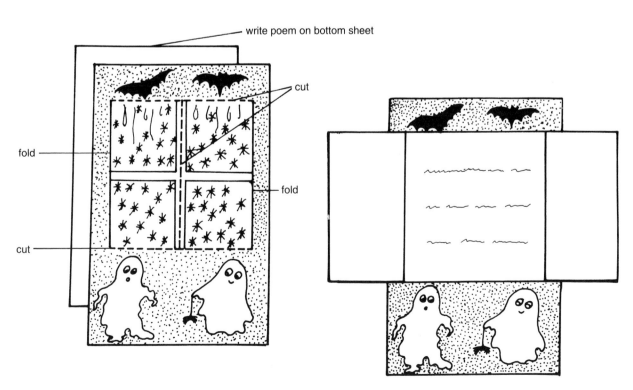

How to make a window poem

21

In the day, people chatter
On their way to work.

At night, they sleep soundly
In their beds.

B Extend the day and night idea to an 'All the day through' poem. Look for words and phrases to express morning and afternoon images and ideas, so that each child or group has four poems, one for each part of the day. Display 'All the day through' on a quartered background, yellow for morning, blue for afternoon, grey for evening, purple for night.

C It might be possible to develop day and night poems into 'Round the clock' poems displayed on two circular backgrounds, each divided into twelve sections. For example:

Round the clock

At midnight, a policeman
walks the empty street.

At one o'clock, an alarm
rips open the silence.

and so on. This is a good way of involving input from all the groups in the class.

D Day and night as a topic provides a good introduction to work on sequence poems, as every child has experience of day following night.

Try sequence poems based on the four seasons of the year. Fold a large sheet of paper into quarters and make up short poems about the town street/playground/apple tree/school garden in each season. Follow the pattern of the poem 'A town street' above, beginning 'In the spring …', 'In summer …' and so on.

Copymaster 8 (What is night?)

A Suggest that children imagine the darkest night. What does it look like? An empty box, the cupboard under the stairs, a black bird, a forest? Children fill in the empty boxes on the copymaster with words and pictures and colour them.

In the first line of the poem at the bottom of the copymaster children should answer the question 'What is night'. For example, 'Night is like … a forest/an empty box/a cupboard under the stairs'.

Then they should add a describing word to go with their idea, thinking of colour, feelings and sounds. If night looks like a forest, children should find an adjective to make the forest sound like night. It might become a *dark* forest, a *dense* forest or a *deep* forest.

The trick now is to extend the original image to include related words and ideas, for example leaves, treetops or shadows, never letting children forget that they are describing night.

Night is like a deep forest
where shadows whisper
in the treetops.

Night is like an empty box
where blackness spills
from corner to corner.

Ask the children to use a different image for night, writing mini-poems of three lines each. Display the poems on a night-time frieze of silhouetted trees and rooftops against a huge white or silver moon.

B Find similar images for day. Is it like the sea? A silk sheet? A gift-wrapped parcel? When children have chosen their image they can use the same three-line pattern to write their poem describing day.

C Make up more image poems following the 'What is night?' pattern on Copymaster 8. Use a three-line format, for example:

A clock is like the face of the moon
where giggling stars tickle
his silver whiskers.

Who's afraid of the dark?

I'm not afraid of the dark, not me –
Hang on, is that a flying bat I see?
A giant moth or a great black bird?
It's the curtain moving, don't be absurd!

What's that shape growing big and fat?
It's not a rhino, I'm sure of that.
A hippopotamus can't get through my door,
There are *no* snakes coiled on my floor.

I'm not afraid of the dark, not me –
I'm as brave as brave can be!
The creature climbing up the wall
Doesn't frighten me at all!

It can't be a spider huge and hairy,
Nor a green-eyed monster wild and scary.
It's not a lizard or a natterjack toad,
Just shadows of trees across the road.

I'm not afraid of the dark, not me –
But I wish Dad would bring my mug of tea!
When I hear his footsteps on the stair
My spooks all vanish into thin air.

I drink my tea and he gives me a hug
And there isn't a sign of beast or bug.
I close my eyes, drift off to sleep,
No ghosts to count, just woolly white sheep!

Moira Andrew

23

June 21st – A day in the life of the sun

Dawn	Rose early.
10 am	Struggled past the low morning cloud.
12 noon	My powerful rays burned long and bright.
4 pm	I kept on shining
6 pm	and shining
8 pm	and shining. I always shine through.
10 pm	Dusk. Late to bed. Slipped down quietly to sleep after a glowing day.

Margaret Blount

Things that go BUMP in the night

Let's make fun of *things that go BUMP in the night!*

List some of the things that frighten you:

bats, ghosts, monsters, snakes ...

Make your poem rhyme, if you can, and make it quite silly!

I see some goggle-eyed bats
and some hairy-monster cats –
But I'm not afraid of the dark,
    not me!

I see _____

and _____
But I'm not afraid of the dark,
    not me!

Copymaster 5

Clock poem

It's eight o'clock! Time for breakfast!

We're all busy,
All the day through!
Can you tell me
The things you do?

It's nine o'clock! Time _____

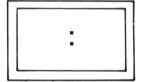

We're all busy,
All the day through!
Can you tell me
The things you do?

It's ten o'clock!   Time _____

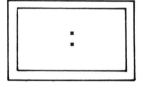

We're all busy,
All the day through!
Can you tell me
The things you do?

It's _____   Time _____

We're all busy,
All the day through!
Can you tell me
The things you do?

It's _____   Time _____

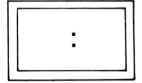

_____
_____
_____

_____

Copymaster 6

Day and night

Day words

sunshine
noise
bright
play
busy

Night words

mysterious
moon
quiet
darkness
sleep

Copymaster 7

What is night?

What does night look like?

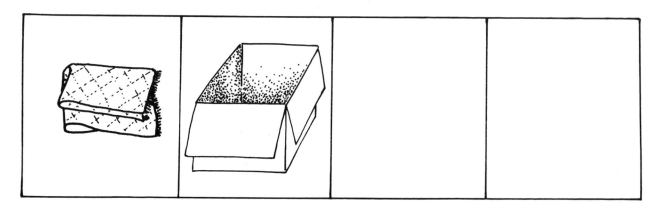

Add a describing word to go with your idea, like this:

Night is like a deep forest

Keep the picture in your mind and write more about it:

Night is like a deep forest
where shadows whisper
    in the treetops.

Write another poem about night.

Night is like _____

Where _____

    in _____

Copymaster 8

FAMILY

The family – of whatever make-up – is an experience common to all children and can be used as a starter for a range of writing: sad, funny, thoughtful, factual and imaginative.

The family has many possibilities for writing, partly because of its familiarity, partly because of its mix of characters and partly because children are permitted to poke fun at brothers and sisters, mums and dads, aunts and uncles, etc.

Copymaster 9 (Growing-up poem)

A This copymaster presents a simple memory list that children can fill in, trying to remember all the things they did – clever, naughty or funny. Begin with talking to the class, perhaps looking at photographs of the children as babies, one-year-olds, two-year-olds and so on. The children might even enjoy looking at photographs of the teacher as a baby! This would give rise to a great deal of excited conversation.

The trick here is to restrict the lines, giving each a similar beat, so that they read like a poem as a whole.

When I was one I splashed in the bath.
When I was two I fell down the stairs.
When I was three I …

Ask children to draw a picture to go with each stage of growing up.

B Use photographs to write portrait poems about different members of the family. Make a concertina book with space for 'portrait' frames on one side, poems on the other.

Copymaster 10 (Who's in trouble now?)

The children will enjoy recalling the times that they, their brothers and sisters, or even Mum or Dad as a child were told off for doing something silly. The longer lines on the copymaster should be filled in with the 'crimes', the shorter ones with the name of the culprit.

An alternative version of this poem can be set in school:

Who dropped a crisp packet in the playground?
Who sat on the newly painted seat?

Darren dropped the crisp bag,
I saw him, I saw him!

Julie sat on the wet paint,
I heard her, I heard her!

and so on, until a class/group poem has been built up. The use of a chorus with a repeat helps the poem along. Encourage the children to think of outrageous ideas to give a surreal quality to the finished piece, for example: 'Who put salt in the caretaker's tea?'.

Copymaster 11 (On the day that I was born)

This is a good follow-up to the growing-up poem. Ask the children to talk to their parents about the weather on the day they were born, what Dad, Grandma, the next-door neighbour said and so on.

Use 'On the day that I was born' as the first line of the poem and fill in the lines on the copymaster. The lines beginning 'So …' are perhaps the most important ones, as they sum up the poem and give it an unusual or unexpected ending; spend time discussing this with the children.

Now get the children to work in pairs to invent the beginnings of ten more lines. They might look like this:

On the day that I was born

An apple tree _____

_____

The doctor said '_____

_____ ,

Encourage the children to exchange line-beginnings with others in the group and finish them off in different ways. Make medals (gold, silver and bronze) and present them, after a judging session for content and style, to the funniest, saddest, most terrifying and most outrageous poets.

Copymaster 12 (Why is Grandad not there?)

A This is a simple conversation poem using questions and answers. However, it can become quite an emotional subject, depending on the answers. If the children decide that Grandad has died, the poem will be quite different to the one in which they say that Grandad is off to the pub!

Take time to talk with the children before letting them use the copymaster. You might uncover some deep questions in the children's minds – but that is often one of the things that poetry does best.

Ask the children to finish off the poem. Suggest that, although it might be sad, it could become a funny poem. Ask a group to find different endings – sad, funny or silly; for example, 'He's gone off with the Martians!'

B Use the idea of conversation to make up a poem. Collect sayings that Grandma, the lady in the corner shop or a funny uncle use. Call the poem 'What my Gran says', 'The things my Uncle Dan says', or even 'What our headteacher says when he's cross!'

I sometimes wonder

I sometimes wonder
what my mum was like
when she was still at school.
Was she, like she says,
as good as gold, or did
she ever play the fool?

I sometimes wonder
if my dad did everything
he was supposed to do.
Did he obey immediately
or did he take his time?
'Not', he says, 'Like you!'

(Meaning me!) One day
I'll ask the grandmamas
if all is as it seems.
I'll get them going
about the good old days
until they spill the beans!

Moira Andrew

If only

If only my mum could
hear herself speak,
'Look at you!' she says.
'You call that washed!
You could grow potatoes
behind those ears!'
Potatoes? If only
it were bags of crisps –
then she'd be talking!

Moira Andrew

Growing-up poem

When I was **one** I _____

When I was **two** I _____

When I was **three** I _____

When I was **four** I _____

When I was **five** I _____

When I was **six** I _____

When I was **seven** I _____

Copymaster 9

Who's in trouble now?

Family

Who let the soap go soggy in the bath?

Who walked mud on the kitchen floor?

_____!

Who _____

Who _____

_____!

Who _____

Who _____

_____!

Copymaster 10

On the day that I was born

Use 'On the day that I was born' as the first line of your poem.

On the day that I was born

The sun _____

_____

My grandfather said ' _____

_____ '

The wind _____

_____

Our neighbour said ' _____

_____ '

So _____

_____

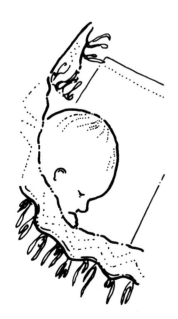

See who can write the funniest, saddest, most terrifying, most outrageous poem.

Copymaster 11

Why is Grandad not there?

I'm going to see Grandma.

Why?

Because she's lonely.

Why?

Because Grandad isn't there.

Why?

Because _____

Why?

Because _____

Why?

Because _____

Why?

Because _____

Why?

Because _____

Can you finish the poem? I expect it will be a sad poem, but you might want to make it funny.

     Copymaster 12

This theme explores the child's world of feelings. It gives children a chance to have their say in a controlled environment – if they are reporting a clash between themselves and Mum they can get their own back without repercussions!

Work through different feelings and give children time to talk about them – when they feel cross/angry/simply furious, and why.

Copymaster 13 (The things people say)

A This copymaster encourages children to listen to the words and phrases people around them use a lot of the time. We are all guilty of over-using particular phrases – as teachers we just have to listen to children playing at schools to hear ourselves speak! On this copymaster, children are actively encouraged to parrot the adults.

Children should first look at the list of words. Some describe the cross face, others the happy face. They can then look for more words to add to each list.

Suggest that each child talks to a partner about things that have happened to make them scowl or stamp, to make them laugh or joke. Perhaps they felt cross when Mum asked them to tidy the bedroom and they would much rather have been on a skateboard or playing a computer game. Perhaps they had a surprise parcel through the post that made them feel happy.

Get the children to make lists of things Mum/Dad/the teacher says when they are cross. The children then make a list of the things they say back – out loud or just inside their heads!

Ask the partners to work together to make a cross mini-poem using the structure provided on the copymaster. Follow this with a happy poem that uses words and phrases from the happy list.

Later, this can be developed into a script for role play that might help children to explore difficult situations. Each mini-script could be worked out differently – some with a happy ending, some funny, some sad. Use the masks you make for Copymaster 15 to help with performance.

B Suggest putting the children's angry/sad/excited phrases in a story or poem written out in comic format with the words in speech balloons. This helps children overcome the problems of where and when to use speech marks and they will enjoy working on this kind of exercise.

Copymaster 14 (I like it when)

A To complete this copymaster the children should think of things that make them feel good. They should then choose four unrelated ideas and write them out on the copymaster. Help the children to cut up their lines,

so that each gets an unusual ending. This gives the finished poem a different, almost surreal feel to it.

B Try a 'I hate it when', 'I'm surprised when' or 'I get angry when' activity and cut up each line in the same way. Make group poems using this idea. Display the 'I like it when' poems on a bright yellow background, angry poems on red, sad poems on blue.

C Make one-poem books using a page for feeling happy/cross/sad. This time, write out each poem using a different colour of felt pen for each emotion.

D Link feelings with colours – red for anger, blue for sadness, yellow for happiness and so on. Make books of feelings poems, each page in a different colour to match the poem.

Make a rainbow of feelings poems to stretch across the classroom (see over).

E Make a feelings spidergram to develop vocabulary.

Copymaster 15 (I'm so angry)

A This copymaster provides a framework for a feelings poem. In it children can be as outrageous as they like!

> I'm so **angry** I could
> Jump on Grandma's smartest hat
> And squash it!
>
> Why?
>
> Because my computer has broken down!

Encourage the children to make their poems full of fun. They can perform them wearing angry/sad/happy masks as shown below. Other feelings can be used to extend the poems.

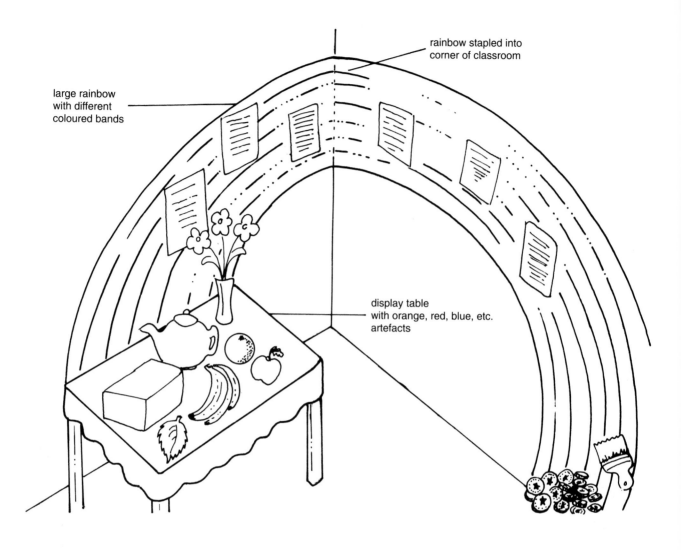

rainbow stapled into corner of classroom

large rainbow with different coloured bands

display table with orange, red, blue, etc. artefacts

A rainbow of feelings poems as a classroom display

B Ask the children to go on a story quest. Encourage them to talk to people at home about something that has made them mad, sad, or excited. Share the story with other children in the group and get everyone to write down one bit of the story. Put the whole thing together as a group poem, taking one line for each idea. Call the poem 'Guess what made Grandad mad!' or '… sad!' or '… happy!'

Copymaster 16 (Poor old …)
In this exercise feelings are given to inanimate objects. Children will need to read or listen to 'The sad bus' from the Anthology on page 37. Use this poem as a writing model to complete the copymaster. The pictures on the copymaster suggest ideas for a 'Poor old car/ boot/house' poem, but it is better if real objects can be examined, either inside or outside the classroom. Look at a redundant computer, a worn-out chair, an inside-out umbrella.

Another way to approach this kind of poem is for the writer to imagine that he or she is the object, for example:

I'm a bus
in the rain
at the end
of the lane.

There are holes
in my side
and my door's
open wide.

My tyres are
shredded and torn,
my seating is patched,
my covers all worn.

Try a range of emotions: an angry bus, a jealous bus, a happy bus. Write out the poems on a bus shape and give each a face expressing sadness, jealousy or joy. (Use Thomas the Tank Engine as a model!) Put the buses in a row inside the bus terminus.

36

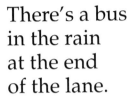

The sad bus

There's a bus
in the rain
at the end
of the lane.

There are holes
in the side
and the door's
open wide,

and it looks
like a very sad bus.

There's a bus
in the rain
that I won't
catch again.

Left for scrap,
rusting, old,
that wet bus
in the cold,

it looks
like a very sad bus.

Ian McMillan

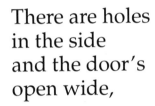
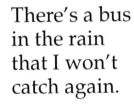

Glad to be alive!

Glad to be alive,
glad to be alive,
I'm glad to be alive
so hit me with five!

I'm a buzzing beehive
who's full of jive.
Full of beans
in my Levi jeans,
with rhythm and beat
jumping out of both feet.
Me, there's no stopping,
I'm snap, crackle, popping.

Glad to be alive,
glad to be alive,
I'm glad to be alive
so hit me with five!

My engine's running,
my acceleration's stunning.
I'm ready for overtaking,
there's no time for braking!
I'm a traffic light who's stuck on green.
Do you know what I mean?
I'm a super,
        duper,
            whooper,
                pooper,
                    little trooper of a guy.
But this spry guy's got to fly so BYE-DEE-BYE!

Ian Souter

The things people say

stamping
scowling
quarrelling

smiling
laughing
joking

Think of the things people say when they are cross and make a cross mini-poem, like this:

'Tidy your room this minute!

Angry mum frowning,
cross child stamping,

_____ mum _____

_____ child _____

'But I like my room in a mess!'

Make a happy poem using the words people say along with words from your happy list.

39   **Copymaster 13**

I like it when

Write about four good things.

I like it when   _____

I like it when   _____

I like it when   _____

I like it when   _____

You might have written:

I like it when the sun is shining,
when I get my maths right,
when my mum smiles at me,
when I stroke the cat's fur ...

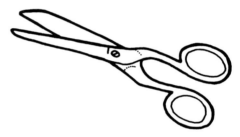

Now make a jumble of your notes:

I like it when my mum   is shining,

when my maths book   smiles at me,

when I stroke   the sunshine ...

Now try a 'I hate it when' poem.

Copymaster 14

I'm so angry

I'm so **angry** I could

_____

_____

Why?

Because _____

_____

I'm so **sad** I could

_____

_____

Why?

Because _____

_____

I'm so **happy** I could

_____

_____

Why?

Because _____

_____

　　　　Copymaster 15

Poor old ...

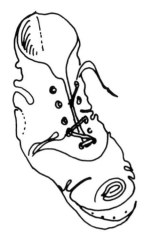

There's a _____

Copymaster 16

GAMES

There is a lot of fun to be had from this topic. Much of the poetry produced will rhyme and it can often be performed as a group – perhaps using percussion instruments as an accompaniment.

Talk about games played in times gone by. A discussion about games makes a good addition to a topic on history.

Copymaster 17 (Build a house)

A The youngest children always enjoy finger rhymes, especially when they can all join in. Perhaps the best known one is:

This is the church.
This is the steeple.
Open the door
And see the people!

Teachers may prefer a secular rhyme these days. 'Build a house' is a new finger rhyme that includes a chorus for performance. Follow the sequence of pictures shown on the copymaster.

B Using 'Build a house' as a pattern, the children can work together to make a new finger rhyme of their own. Try:

Paint a portrait,
paint a portrait,
paint it all in red.
Splash it on my hands,
spill it on my head!

Paint a portrait,
paint a portrait,
paint it all in blue.
Splash it on my feet,
just see what I can do!

Mime a portrait frame in the air with both hands, then 'paint' up and down, touch hands and head and so on.

C Try 'Dig a hole', 'Climb, climb the mountain high' or 'Let's bake a Christmas (birthday) cake!' Perhaps a group of children could make up percussion rhythms to play while others are chanting or singing the poems.

D Collect playground rhymes, skipping rhymes, counting rhymes and so on. As a handwriting exercise, these can be put together, illustrated and gathered into a class book of games. (See Iona and Peter Opie's book *The Lore and Language of School Children*, OUP, 1967.)

E Ask parents and grandparents about games they played when they were children. Write stories and poems with the title 'When I was a child'. Make illustrated books.

F Collect ideas for games to play at Christmas time. Write them out and put them together in a Christmas book. These can be sold at the Christmas fair to help your favourite school charity.

G As a design/writing exercise discuss how a complicated playground game is played. Then ask children to write it out (with diagrams, if necessary) so that other children can play it and understand the rules. This exercise tests the children's ability to write in a precise, technical style.

Try out the children's skills by exchanging games ideas with a parallel class in another school. Can the recipients work out how to play the game from the written/illustrated instructions?

Copymaster 18 (Pass the parcel)
This is a poem based on the familiar party game. Ask the children to suggest two things about each parcel, including colour. For example: 'A blue, stripy parcel', 'A green, spotty parcel' or 'A round, red parcel'. Colour the parcels on the copymaster. In the final box, draw the prize found in the last parcel.

Make a double concertina book with parcels cut and folded as opening flaps to conceal their presents underneath (see below). To create a vivid class display, make a series of coloured boxes to look like parcels (complete with poem) and hang them up as mobiles (see over).

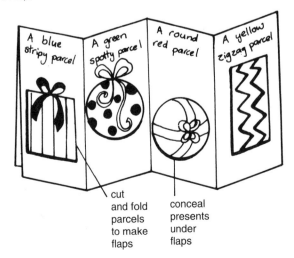

A parcel concertina book

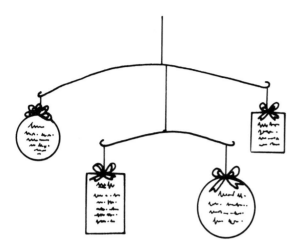

A parcel mobile

Copymaster 19 (What can you do with a ball?)
A 'filling-in' vocabulary exercise. Children will have to think hard to come up with the wide range of verbs required. In addition, a rhyme is needed if the pattern is to be followed, although this is not essential. Neologisms (made-up words) can be used.

The completed poem works well as a performance piece, perhaps involving catching or bouncing balls. (Practice will be required!) Poems can be displayed on different types of balls hung from the ceiling.

The pattern 'What can you do with ...' can also be used with many other subjects, both serious and funny.

Copymaster 20 (Magic carpet)
The children should have access to a globe or world atlas for this task. Bring in holiday brochures and talk about exciting parts of the world they might like to visit – no passports or tickets necessary, no expense spared! The magic carpet will take them anywhere they choose. Discuss climate, scenery and food, and the adventures the children might have.

Suggest that the children draw some of the places they would like to visit. Find three more words in addition to the ones on the copymaster to describe how the magic carpet moves. Use them, together with the other ideas you have discussed, to fill in the spaces on the copymaster and a poem will take shape. Ask the children to write more verses using the same structure.

Display individual poems on coloured 'flying carpets' and paste them collage-style onto a frieze of outer space with the earth just visible on the lower edge (see below).

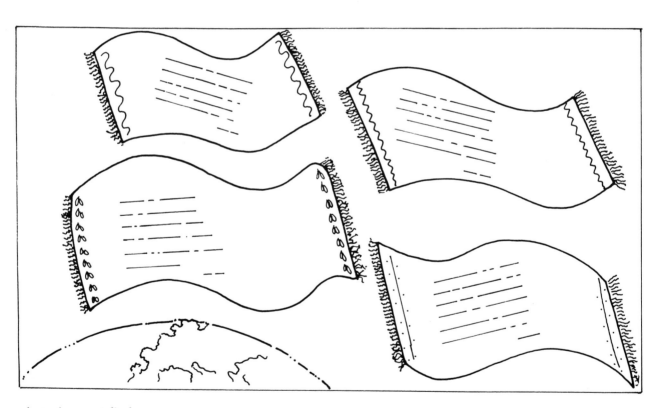

A magic carpet display

On our side of the playground

On our side of the playground
It's hand-stands against the wall,
Or noisy games of rounders
Or skipping or netball.

On their side of the playground
It's football or marbles or such,
Or Space Ships or 'Oggy 'Oggy
Or British Bulldog or Touch.

But when we go on their side
And try to steal their ball,
Then that's the very bestest game
We ever have of all!

John Cotton

No score

Peter passes to Jenny,
    Jenny passes to Paul,
        Paul hits a header to Simon,
            But Simon misses the ball!
                Susie right there (she's the sweeper)
                    Shoot! she hears the crowd call,
                        She shoots at the goal – and she misses!
We haven't scored at all!

David Orme

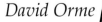

Build a house

Build a house,
Build a house,
Build a house of wood!
Bang goes the hammer
To make it strong and good!

Push out your elbows to make the ground.

Touch your elbows to make the walls.

Four fingers to make the chimneys.

Here comes the wind!

Blow, blow ... one chimney gone!

Blow, blow ... two chimneys gone!

Blow, blow ... three chimneys gone!

Blow, blow ... four chimneys gone!

Blow, blow ... down go the walls!

Build a house,
Build a house,
Build a house of wood!
Bang goes the hammer
To make it strong and good!

Copymaster 17

 **Pass the parcel**

Pass the parcel, round and round!
Tear off the paper, and what have you found?

A _____ _____ parcel

Pass the parcel, round and round!
Tear off the paper, and what have you found?

A _____ _____ parcel

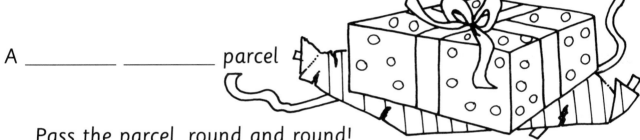

Pass the parcel, round and round!
Tear off the paper, and what have you found?

A _____ _____ parcel

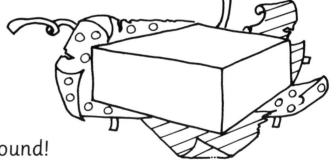

Pass the parcel, round and round!
Tear off the paper, and what have you found?

A _____ !

47   **Copymaster 18**

What can you do with a ball?

You can ...
kick it,
whack it,
head it
and smack it!

_____ it
shoot it

_____ it
and boot it!

_____ it

_____ it

_____ it

and _____ it!

There are ...
Hard red cricket balls
Black and white footballs

_____ tennis balls

_____ _____ balls

Keep them bouncing, all the day,
Football, netball, who wants to play?

Copymaster 19

Magic carpet

Imagine if your bed was a magic carpet.
Draw some of the places you'd like to visit.

sailing   *soaring*   *flying*

_____   _____   _____

My magic carpet goes _____

over the mountains, across the seas

to _____

where _____

And I can see _____

I can see _____

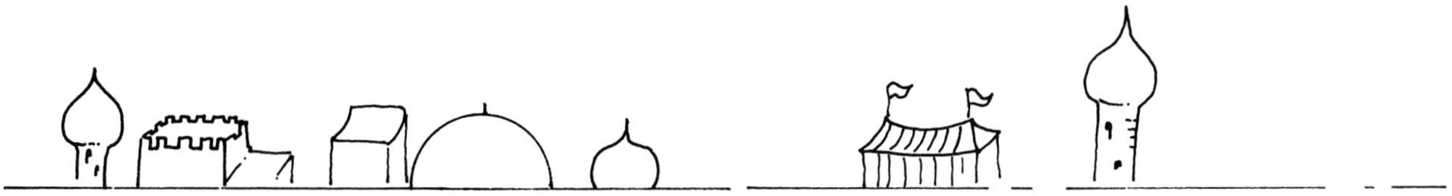

My magic carpet goes _____

over the mountains, across the seas

to _____

where _____

And I can hear _____

I can hear _____

Can you write more?

Copymaster 20

NUMBERS

Poems with a number sequence give a structure to writing and performing, and reinforce number concepts. There are many well-known counting and finger rhymes to introduce to children. Many excellent ones will be found in *This Little Puffin* (Elizabeth Matterson, Puffin Books, 1969).

Popular counting rhymes include:

Five currant buns in the baker's shop
Round and fat with sugar on the top.
Along came [child's name] with a penny one day
Bought a currant bun and took it away.

One, two, three four five
Once I caught a fish alive.
Which finger did it bite?
This little finger on the right.

Ten fat sausages, sizzling in the pan,
One went POP and the other went BANG!

Find the poems that count forward and back, and count in twos. Counting forward can result in accumulating poems. A chorus line can be added for extra effect:

What did we buy, what did we buy,
What did we buy today?

One loaf of bread.

What did we buy, what did we buy,
What did we buy today?

One loaf of bread,
Two red tomatoes.

What did we buy, what did we buy,
What did we buy today?

One loaf of bread,
Two red tomatoes,
Three ...

Copymaster 21 (Three)
Three is a 'magic' number – three bears, three wishes, three billy-goats Gruff, three kings and so on. Cut along the flaps on the copymaster then paste it onto a backing sheet.

For three wishes, write one wish under each flap. Encourage wishes that are not merely acquisitive, but that also have interesting language possibilities. Here is one idea:

First wish: what I would like to see.
Second wish: what I would like to hear.
Third wish: what I would like to taste.

Animal poems are another possibility. For 'Three cats', for example, write little descriptions of one cat under each flap.

I'm a ginger cat. I like catching mice!
I'm a white cat. I like ...
I'm a tabby cat. I like ...

Copymaster 22 (What's in Peter's pocket?)
Here children have to write their own counting poem in the space on the copymaster. Possibilities include: ...'s bedroom; the teacher's desk; the secret cupboard; the mysterious night garden; the sweet shop; the dustbin.

Use number mobiles for these poems. The mobiles can also be useful for first/second/ third (ordinal) counting poems.

Copymaster 23 (Think of a million)
Cut round the cover of the book on the copymaster, then mount it on a backing sheet cut to the same size. Talk about very big numbers. Ask each child to finish the sentence 'A million is ...' inside their own book, with suitable pictures. For example:

A million is
The stars on a cold winter night
Winking at the moon.

Copymaster 24 (How many?)
This copymaster provides a structure for thinking about the concept 'how many'. A simple version is to decide on suitable numbers, perhaps increasing each time:

How many children in the class?
      Thirty!
How many children in the town?
      A thousand!
How many children in the world?

and so on. The numbers will be guessed if they are big. A more sophisticated version would include a response to the question on the copymaster, prompting another question, another response and so on.

How many bees are buzzing in the hive?
As many as daisies in the long grass.

How many daisies are in the long grass?
As many as ...

This makes a chain poem that can return to the first idea (the bees) to close the chain.

Ten red geraniums

Ten red geraniums
sprouting when it's fine,
a slug came slithering
and then there were nine.

Nine red geraniums
glowing when it's late,
a bat came blundering
and then there were eight.

Eight red geraniums
shining bright as heaven,
a magpie moth came munching
and then there were seven.

Seven red geraniums
propped up by sticks,
a wire worm came wriggling
and then there were six.

Six red geraniums
fiery and alive,
a weevil came wandering
and then there were five.

Five red geraniums
dancing by the door,
a beetle came biting
and then there were four.

Four red geraniums
as vivid as can be,
a caterpillar came crawling
and then there were three.

Three red geraniums
petals all brand new,
a ladybird came lunching
and then there were two.

Two red geraniums
blazing in the sun,
a great aunt came admiring
and then there was one.

One red geranium –
the only one I've got,
I'll keep it on my window sill
in its own well-watered pot.

Moira Andrew

Three

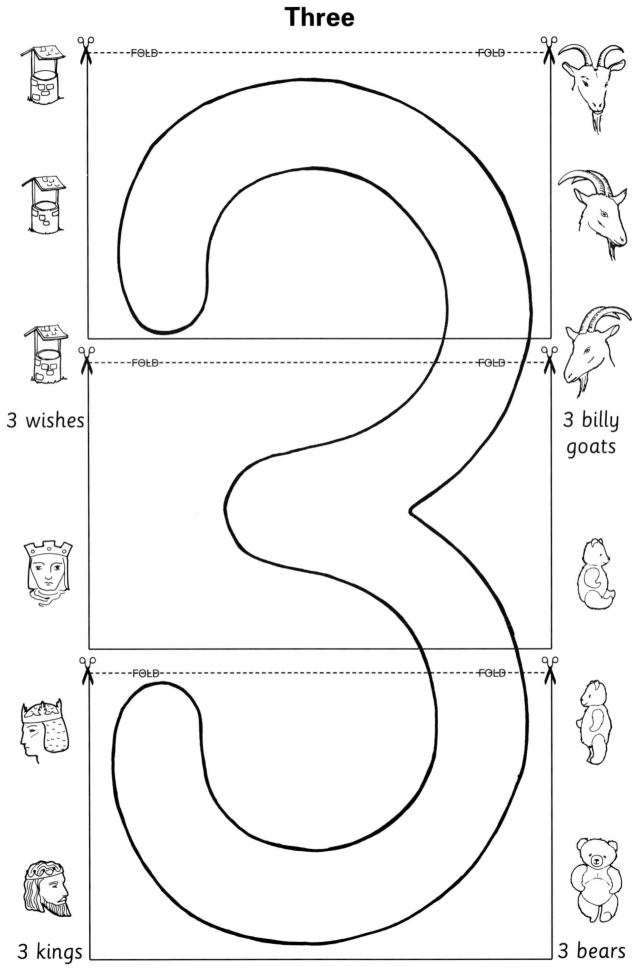

3 wishes

3 billy goats

3 kings

3 bears

52

Copymaster 21

What's in Peter's pocket?

What's in _____

_____

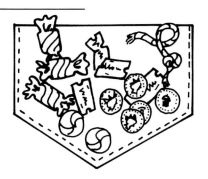

1 piece of knotty string,
2 marbles, orange and blue,
3 peppermints in a packet
4 crumpled bus tickets
5 shiny pennies to spend!

1 _____

2 _____

3 _____

4 _____

5 _____

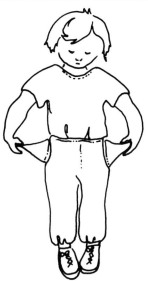

53

Copymaster 22

Think of a million

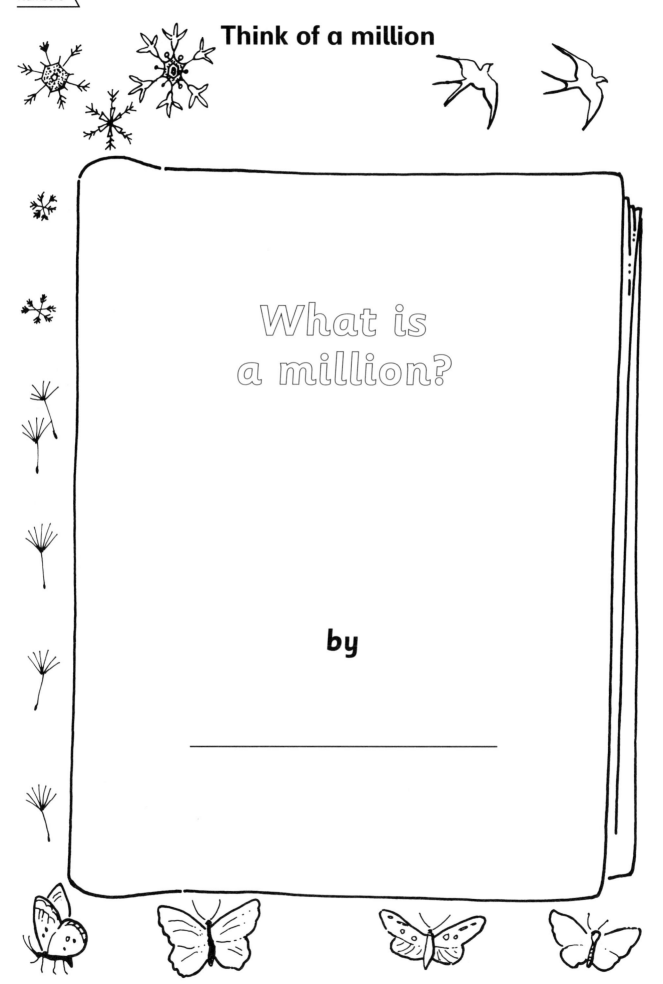

What is
a million?

by

_____

Copymaster 23

How many?

How many bees are buzzing in the hive?

How many _____ are _____

In the _____

How many _____ are _____

In the _____

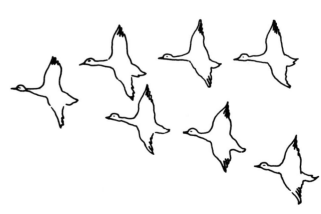

Copymaster 24

SEASONS

The theme of seasons is always topical. Writing about the way in which the year turns helps children to develop a sense of wonder, look closely at changes in the natural world, listen and observe as scientists, and write and draw as artists.

The seasons offer a rich seam for teacher and pupil to mine alike. Use changes in the weather, trees, garden colour, length of day, animal and bird life, playground games and so on as starter possibilities.

Teachers who expect children to write a poem on spring, without offering a pattern or helping them to organise their ideas, expect the impossible! True, some will turn out excellent work, but most children respond best to some form of structured help and these copymasters on seasons are designed to give young poets success.

Copymaster 25 (Christmas counting poem)
This counting poem offers a new way to tell the familiar Christmas story. It is a good pattern to work on with a whole class or group. Elements of the story that might be included are camels, oxen, donkeys, shepherds, children, sheep, angels – enough possibilities to involve everyone.

When it is finished, the poem can serve as a simple nativity play for the youngest children. The chorus line can be extended or words from a favourite carol substituted.

Make the poem into a book with the words on the left-hand page, pictures on the right. Another method of displaying the poem is to cut the book into a stable shape, with a decreasing number of characters in the stable as the pages are turned. The final page should show:

Two loving parents, Mary and Joseph
One baby Jesus smiling and playing
All in the stable on Christmas Day.

Copymaster 26 (Recipe for winter)

A First 'collect' the ingredients – snow, ice, frost, bare trees, snowmen, cold winds and so on; add some winter colours and winter pastimes. Get the children to suggest ideas orally, then make a written list from which to choose. This helps those who find writing difficult, yet allows the more confident to use their own ideas.

Follow the recipe form to build up the poem on the copymaster. The first two verses might look like this:

Take some deep white snow,
some bright slippery ice
and a pale yellow moon.

Add some red holly berries,
some bare black trees
and some whirling snowflakes.

When the poems are finished, make up a recipe book for winter.

Display individual poems on a dark frieze decorated with white or silver snowflakes (shown below) or frame each one with a winter scene, edged with silver ink or paint.

B Divide the class into four groups. Ask each group to choose a different season and then brainstorm ideas related to it. They might think about: what sort of person the season is (spring might be a baby); what colour clothes it would wear; what its favourite food might be; what hobbies it would have and so on. These ideas can be worked on to produce poems personifying each season. Use them in a dramatic performance or for a circular seasons display (see opposite).

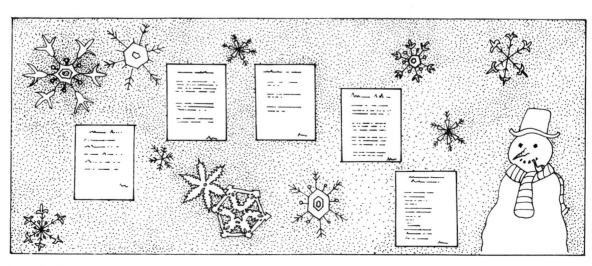

A winter display

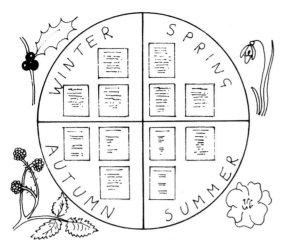

A circular seasons display

Display the image poem on a spiral as shown below.

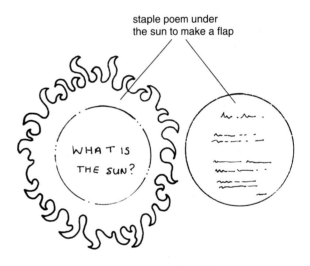

A spiral display

Alternatively, write it out on a circle of coloured paper and staple another on top to make a secret flap that the reader has to open.

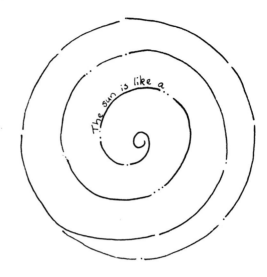

Displaying the image poem under a flap

C Make up love/hate poems based on the seasons: For example:

I like winter because …
But I hate summer because …

I like spring because …
But I hate autumn because …

I like summer because …
But I hate winter because …

D Build up poetry calendars using the characteristics of each month. Use the poems on a class calendar.

E Follow the recipe pattern to make up a poem for each season or, indeed, as a way of writing about each of the twelve months.

Copymaster 27 (What is the sun?)
A This poem works best if it is built up on the 'shopping list' principle. Ask children to close their eyes and visualise the sun – colour, shape and place. They then open their eyes and think about toys that look like the sun – a yellow ball, a golden frisbee, an orange balloon and so on. The poem helps the children to think in image, which is a very important skill in a poet's development.

Write some of the suggestions on the blackboard. It is a good idea to list only three ideas – too many make it difficult for children to choose for themselves. Make a list of three foods that look like the sun (for example an orange, pancake, Rich Tea biscuit) and three flowers (for example a marigold, buttercup, sunflower).

Ask the children to choose two ideas and draw and colour them in the empty boxes on the copymaster. Now choose words to describe the way a balloon/ball/frisbee moves (for example floating, bouncing and whizzing). Think about how to describe where the sun is (for example in the sky, in the air, in space or above the clouds). Ask the children to write their choices in the spaces provided.

Encourage the children to use the ideas on their list to build up the rest of the 'What is the sun?' poem, following the pattern on the copymaster.

B Build more image poems, based on the weather – for example wind, rain, snow. These can be very effective and help children towards using and understanding simile and metaphor.

Copymaster 28 (Springtime eggs)
Talk about creatures other than birds that hatch from eggs – for example snakes, reptiles and snails. Paste the finished poem onto the egg shape on the copymaster, then cut out the completed 'eggs' and mount in a basket or a nest to make a class/group display. Alternatively, colour the eggshell completely and 'hide' the poem underneath as in 'What is the sun?' Another option is to describe the creature on the top and make a drawing of it underneath.

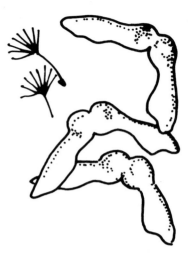

Autumn treasure

Seeds on the wind
travelling in the air,
seeds on parachutes
twirling everywhere.

Seeds from pepperpots
shaken on the ground,
seeds like catapults
shooting all around.

Seeds bright as jewels,
seeds on the wing,
seeds buried in the earth
ready for the spring.

Moira Andrew

Summertime

Cows paddle deep
in buttercups,
like fat aunties
wading into waves
at the seaside.

Moira Andrew

Christmas counting poem

What is in the stable on Christmas Day?

Eight _____

Seven _____

All in the stable on Christmas Day.

Six _____

Five _____

All in the stable on Christmas Day.

Four _____

Three wise kings, carrying gifts,

All in the stable on Christmas day.

Two loving parents, Mary and Joseph

One baby Jesus _____

All in the stable on Christmas day.

Copymaster 25

 **Recipe for winter**

snow   _____   _____

grey   _____   _____

bare trees   _____   _____

sledging   _____   _____

Recipe for winter

Take some deep white snow,

some _____

and _____

Add some red holly berries,

some _____

and _____

Mix with days of silver frost,

some _____

and _____

Decorate with _____

some _____

and _____

Leave in the freezer
for three long months
and you have made *WINTER!*

What is the sun?

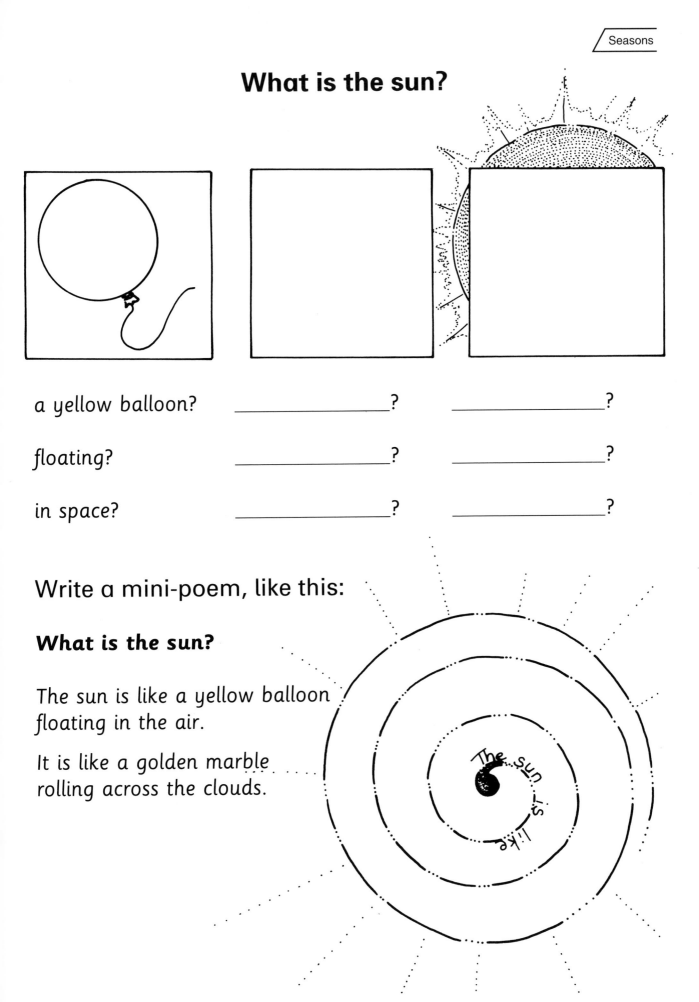

a yellow balloon?   _____?   _____?

floating?   _____?   _____?

in space?   _____?   _____?

Write a mini-poem, like this:

What is the sun?

The sun is like a yellow balloon
floating in the air.

It is like a golden marble
rolling across the clouds.

Make up another poem, this time about the rain.

61

Springtime eggs

I'm just
a sparrow,
But give me some
crumbs and I'll be
A washing-line
tightrope walker or
An early morning
pop star!

What's hatching
from the egg?

Talk about creatures that hatch from eggs.
What is in your egg?

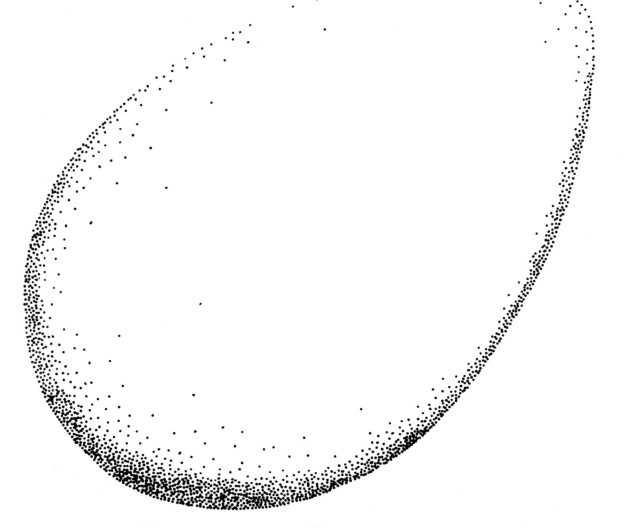

Copymaster 28

WHEELS

Transport is a popular topic in the primary school curriculum, but 'Wheels' can also be used to introduce writing work on a range of other sequential themes, such as 'Seasons', 'Round the clock', 'A journey to town and back', or 'Through the week: Monday to Sunday'.

Use 'Wheels' as the basis of a transport topic, but enlarge the possibilities into other thematic work. Take the idea into PE and dance, making up rhythmic choruses to match.

Copymaster 29 (Many wheels)

A This copymaster uses Maggie Holmes' poem 'Sing a song of many wheels' as a model (Anthology, page 65). Discuss different kinds of wheels and their uses with the children before reading the poem. List their ideas, then read the poem aloud. If preferred, the original poem can be kept under wraps until the children have drafted their own writing. Their ideas will probably be in simple two-line statements, for example:

Huge tractor wheels
Grinding through the mud.

Steel train wheels
Clattering through the tunnel.

Each child should add his or her verse. Add percussion and build the poem into a performance.

B Make a display table of all kinds of wheels: watch wheels, toy-car wheels, pram wheels, a steering wheel and so on, arranged in order of size from the smallest to the largest you can accommodate.

Put up pictures and posters of other types of wheel (for example water wheels, windmills, Ferris wheels) and add books to the display table, open at appropriate pages, showing cars, trains, tractors, etc. Encourage the children to look for wheel poems in class/school resources. Make an anthology, with published poems used alongside the children's own.

Copymaster 30 (Wheelspokes)

Each spoke on the copymaster has room for one line of a poem, making an eight-line poem. The wheels can be put together as either a group or class display. Use the pattern for poems about the seasons, so that they are cyclical. For example:

Spring is painted white with snowdrops,
pink with blossom, yellow with daffodils.

Summer is painted green with new leaves,
blue with irises, scarlet with poppies.

Autumn is painted ...
...

Winter is painted ...
...

An attractive option is to photocopy the wheelspokes onto card, or cut them out and mount them on card. Put a paper fastener through the centre of the wheel so that it will revolve.

Copymaster 31 (Weather wheel)

A This idea is based on Moira Andrew's poem in the Anthology on page 66. Ask the children to think of events that happen in the four seasons, finding two-word ideas. For example: 'seeds scatter', 'earth kisses', 'snow ...'. Brainstorm and fill in appropriate verbs for 'roots', 'seedlings' and 'stems' for the spring section on the copymaster. Work on the autumn, winter and summer sections in the same way.

B Use the wheel for a 'Round the clock' poem, talking about what might happen each hour of the day and night. Make up a three-line poem, for example:

At one o'clock the church clock chimes,
    Boom,
and the cats walk walls like shadows.

At two o'clock the church clock chimes,
    Boom Boom,
and the children sleep sound in their beds.

and so on. This again makes a performance poem with a chorus, the youngest children enjoying the 'Boom' part – especially in the final verse at twelve o'clock!

Display the poem inside a huge wheel on the classroom wall.

Copymaster 32 (Wheel rhythms)

A Let children think of a rhythm to fit car tyres, bus wheels, train wheels, a road roller and so on, using the copymaster as a prompt. Build up a poem following the pattern below.

Zippety zap go the car wheels
    rolling along the wet road,
        zippety zap, zippety zap
            zippety zap, zipping off
                into the distance ...

Clickety clack go the train wheels,
    running along the steel track,
        clickety clack, clickety clack,
            clickety clack, clicking off
                into the distance ...

Make this poem into a performance, with voices getting softer and softer until they fade away at the end off 'into the distance'. Use percussion instruments to add to the effect of this poem.

The youngest children enjoy moving along to the poem, arms and legs working in time to the rhythms.

B Write fairground poems, using a rhythmic pattern. For example:

Round and round goes the Big Wheel,
    Round and round goes our car.
Round and round goes the Big Wheel,
    The ground looks ever so far!

Round and round goes the roundabout,
    Up and down we go really fast.
Round and round goes the roundabout,
    Mum and Dad wave as we pass.

Let the children make up more verses about the fair, using the same rhythmic pattern. Display a class poem with brightly painted wheels and roundabouts, or individual poems inside coloured circles, decorated and patterned with felt-tip pens or oil-based pastels.

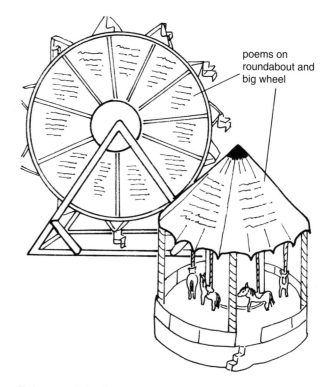

poems on roundabout and big wheel

Fairground display

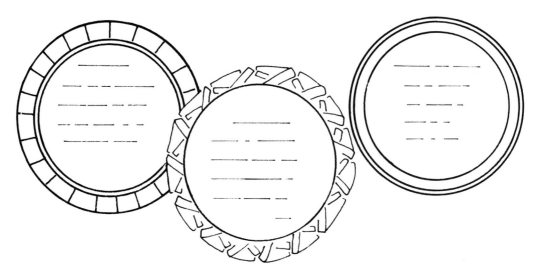

Class display of individual poems on wheels

64

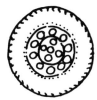
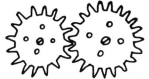

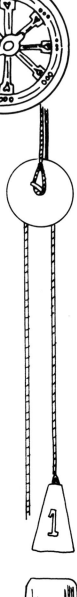

Sing a song of many wheels

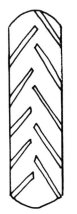

Sing a song of turning wheels
Spinning round and round,
Motor bikes and bus wheels
Roll along the ground.

Screeching wheels and rumbling tyres
Rotating fast and slow,
Splashing through the puddles
Or leaving tread marks in the snow.

Wheel and deal for tyres and wheels
Punctured, slashed and torn.
They end up on the scrap heap,
Used and bald and worn.

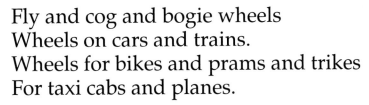

Fly and cog and bogie wheels
Wheels on cars and trains.
Wheels for bikes and prams and trikes
For taxi cabs and planes.

Pulley wheels at pit heads
Lifting up the coal.
Clanking wheels on wagons,
Hear the coal trucks roll.

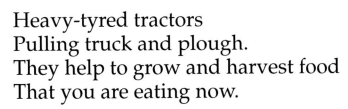

Heavy-tyred tractors
Pulling truck and plough.
They help to grow and harvest food
That you are eating now.

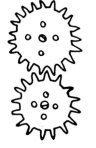

Sing a song of many wheels
Turning round and round.
Can you think of other wheels
That I may not have found?

Maggie Holmes

(Start at any point and work clockwise.)

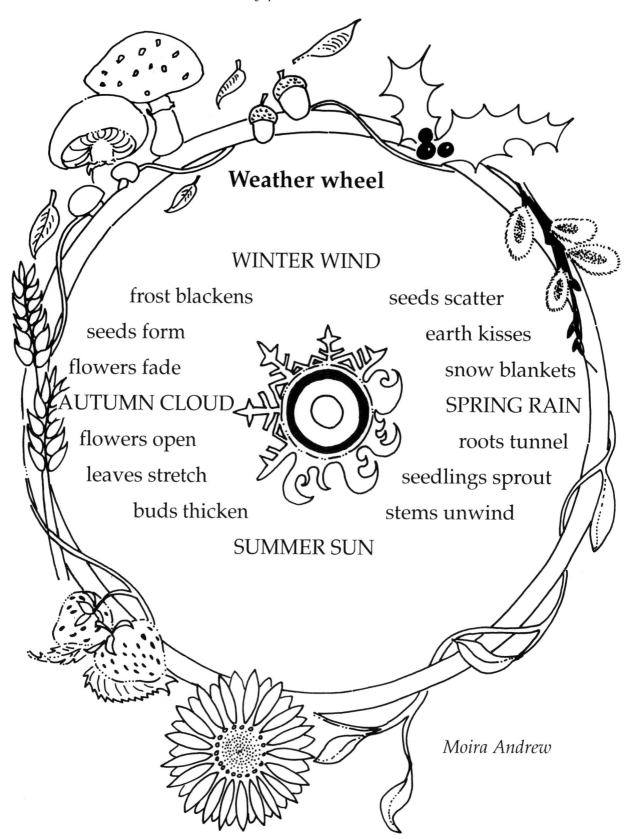

Weather wheel

WINTER WIND

frost blackens   seeds scatter

seeds form   earth kisses

flowers fade   snow blankets

AUTUMN CLOUD   SPRING RAIN

flowers open   roots tunnel

leaves stretch   seedlings sprout

buds thicken   stems unwind

SUMMER SUN

Moira Andrew

Many wheels

Sing a song of many wheels
spinning round and round,
can you think of other wheels
that I may not have found?

_____

_____

_____

_____

_____

_____

Sing a song of many wheels
spinning round and round
listen to the sorts of wheels

that _____ has found!

Copymaster 29

Wheelspokes

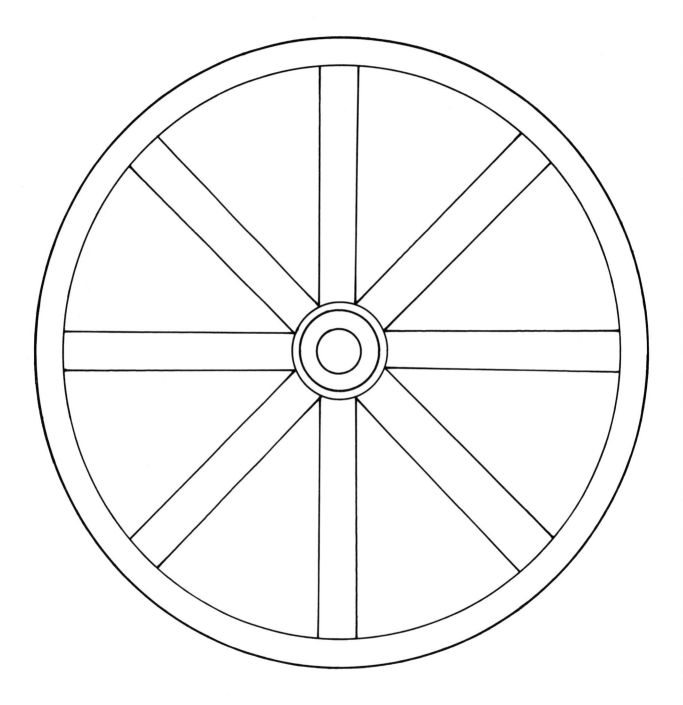

Copymaster 30

Weather wheel

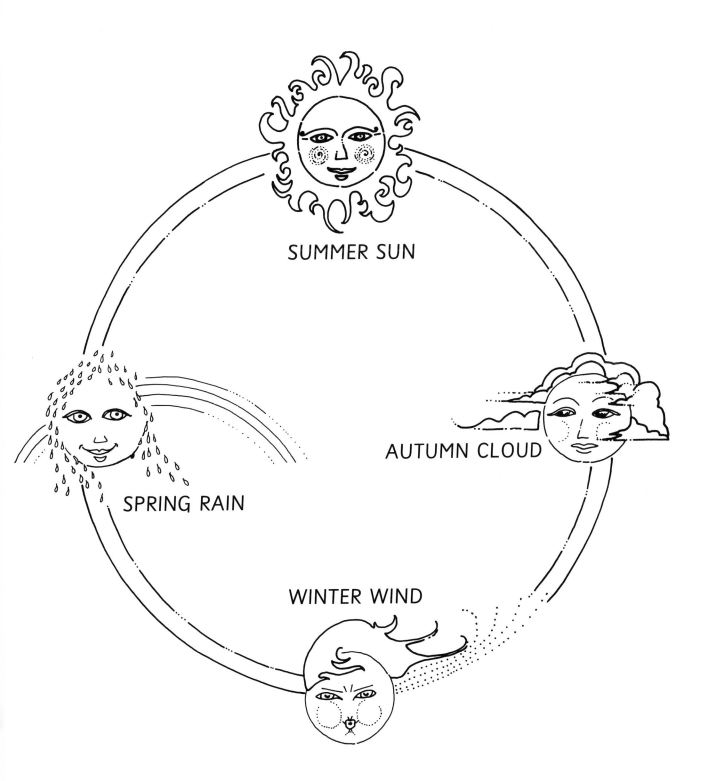

SUMMER SUN

SPRING RAIN

AUTUMN CLOUD

WINTER WIND

Copymaster 31

Wheel rhythms

Listen to these rhythms.
What sort of wheels might make these rhythms?
Make up your own rhythm and put it in the box.

Zippety zip, zippety zap!
Zippety zip, zippety zap!

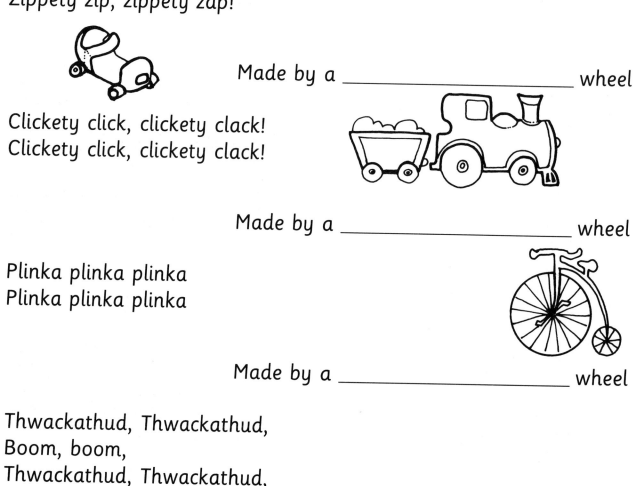

Made by a _____ wheel

Clickety click, clickety clack!
Clickety click, clickety clack!

Made by a _____ wheel

Plinka plinka plinka
Plinka plinka plinka

Made by a _____ wheel

Thwackathud, Thwackathud,
Boom, boom,
Thwackathud, Thwackathud,
Boom, boom,

Made by a _____ wheel

Made by a _____ wheel

Copymaster 32

WIND AND STORM

While wind is a topic particularly relevant for March, it is useful throughout the year as it is so immediate. The children can experience wind through their senses and, in addition, it has the magic quality of being invisible – this has enormous appeal to children.

Use some of the wind-poem ideas as ways of beginning work on other weather poems.

Copymaster 33 (Wind kennings)

A A kenning is an unusual way of describing something, a compound word that encapsulates a property of the thing in question. The poem below is made up of water kennings:

A fire-drowner
A snow-melter
A loo-flusher
A body-cooler
A plant-refresher
A fish-breather
A fountain-sprayer
A wave-crasher

Use the same idea for wind kennings. Encourage the children to think through the idea of wind so that they can come up with new descriptions, ones that are apt and that capture the essence of it. The copymaster includes a couple of prompts and space for the children's own ideas. Children can have a lot of fun with this way of writing. Encourage group to play against group to see who can come up with the best descriptions.

B The finished wind kennings can be strung together to make a series of flags using cut-outs from the enlarged copymaster or flags made in class. Display them across the hall or, for maximum effect, mount them on material, tie them to the branches of a tree in the school garden and let them blow in the wind. Infants also enjoy running in the wind waving these wind poems behind them.

C Work on a sun kenning, a snow kenning and a rain kenning.

Copymaster 34 (Weather riddle)

A Weather makes a good subject for a riddle. Ask the children to choose a wild animal as fierce as the winter wind. Ask them to imagine that they have turned into the animal they have chosen. Encourage the children to answer questions in the animal's persona. Are you a bear? A wolf? Where do you live? How do you move? What sounds can you make?

Make up a riddle on the board with the children's help. Show them that a riddle is a poem puzzle. The children have to make up clues, but try to hide the identity of the weather. The structure below is easy for children to follow.

I am like a wolf	(creature)
hiding in the forest.	(place)
I howl in the night.	(sound)
I can tear your hat off.	(action)
What am I?	(question)

In the blank box on the copymaster, children can draw the creature that their weather is like. They then write the riddle in the space below. When the children have written their riddles, give them a square of paper folded as shown below. Use the outside as the cover with the title and author's name. Write the riddle inside and hide the answer to the riddle beneath a flap.

B Write more weather riddles using the pattern above. Display the riddles inside one-poem books, as suggested above.

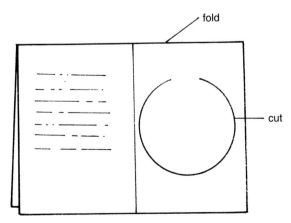

Weather riddle book

Copymaster 35 (Stormy weather)

A Listen to the sound of the wind on a stormy day. Look at what it does to trees, leaves and flowers. Look at the way people have to bend into the wind to walk. Think how safe and warm one feels, inside looking out.

Find more inside-looking-outside words and write them into the spaces in the top half of the copymaster. Help the children to make lists of things they can see and hear in a storm. Use the ideas from the list to fill in the spaces in the bottom half of the copymaster and a poem will grow. Now think of a child who is outside looking in and make another poem in the same way.

Display the 'Stormy weather' poems behind a 'window'. Write the poem neatly in the middle of A4 paper. Put a second sheet on top, cut and folded as shown below to make a window that opens to reveal the poem beneath. Use coloured pencil very lightly to draw tossing trees and whirling leaves behind the words of the poem.

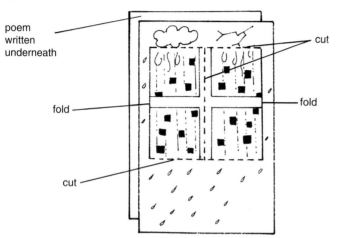
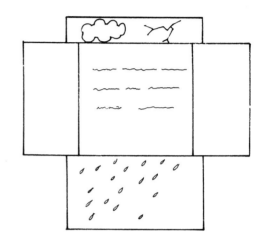

Making a 'Stormy weather' window

B Keep a weather diary showing day-to-day weather. Make up rhymes to go with different weathers and make a class book of weather poems.

C Build up a list of wind-sound images:

A howling wolf
A wailing ghost
A crashing wave
A cat rustling through the grass
A burglar rattling the windows
A dragon breathing fire

and so on. Put them in order of violence and perform the sound poem with a percussion accompaniment.

D Find as many traditional weather rhymes as you can, for example:

Mist in May, heat in June,
Makes the harvest come right soon.

Gather them together into an illustrated book of weather.

Copymaster 36 (Kites)
The poem 'Wind' in the Anthology on page 73 uses the technique of syllable counting, with lines increasing and then decreasing in numbers of syllables. Sometimes this can be a difficult idea to convey to young children, so a good way to begin is to get them to beat out their own names on percussion instruments. Make a group of children with one-syllable names (Tom, Sam, Sue), another with two-syllable names (Kelly, David, Asha), then three (Kusuma, Katherine, Natalie) and so on.

Move on to counting the syllables of objects around the classroom before working on words to go with the wind. Help the children to work out how 'Wind' is constructed. Work with the children to make up another poem on the board to fit the growing syllable-count pattern. Let them copy it out on the second kite shape on the copymaster.

Some of the children might like to have a go on their own. Let them complete the poem in the first kite on the copymaster. For example:

It
started
in the trees
but soon the wind
made all the leaves dance
leaving the branches bare
storm-tossed like ships on the sea

Display the wind-syllable poems on coloured kites, made from cut-outs from the enlarged copymaster or in the classroom hanging from the ceiling. Knot bright ribbons onto the strings to make an attractive and colourful class display.

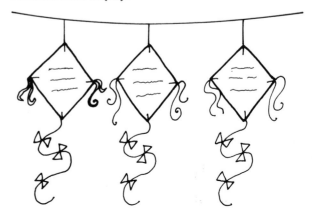

Wind

It
Started
As a breeze
But soon the gusts
Were chasing dead leaves,
Making waves on the pond,
Clattering letterboxes,
Pushing umbrellas inside out,
Trying to rip branches off the trees.

At last the wind is dying down,
But before it fades away
It gives one last great roar
Through the letterbox;
Now we go out
tidy up.
What a
mess!

David Orme

Racing the wind

eyes staring
nostrils flaring

feet dancing
legs prancing

manes flowing
tails blowing

hooves pacing
horses racing

Moira Andrew

Wind kennings

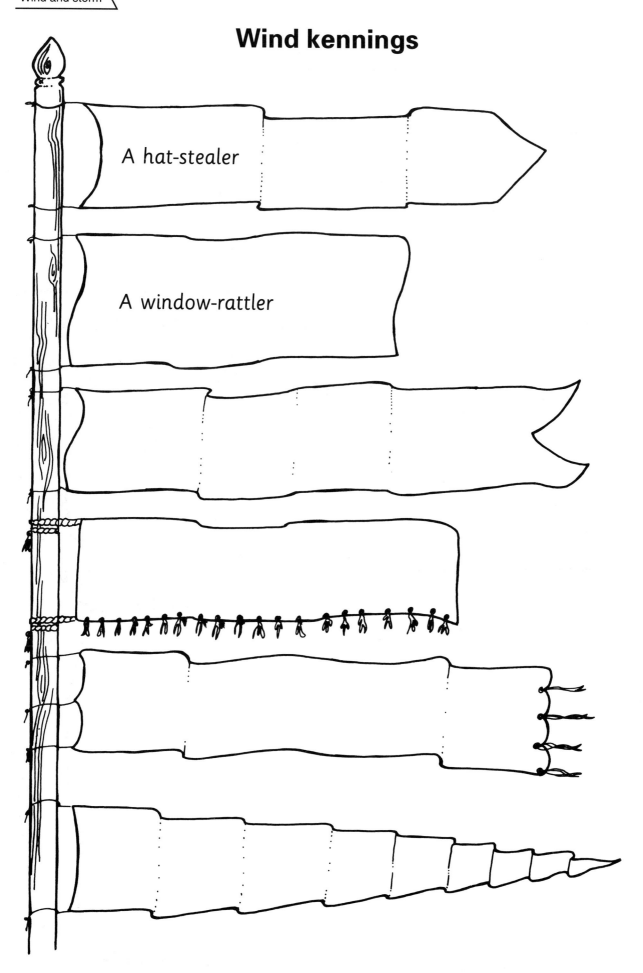

A hat-stealer

A window-rattler

Copymaster 33

Weather riddle

Write a poem as if you are the wind, but try to hide who you are, so that your poem is a puzzle.

It might look like this:

I am a ghost	(creature)
haunting the forest.	(place)
I sing a creepy song.	(sound)
I will chase you home.	(action)
What am I?	(question)

75

Copymaster 34

Stormy weather

safe

warm

_____

_____

dangerous

cold

_____

_____

I am inside,
looking outside
at the raging storm.

I see_____

some_____

and _____

But I am inside,
looking outside
at the raging storm.

I hear_____

some_____

and _____

But I am inside,
looking outside
at the raging storm.

I am outside,
looking inside
at the child in bed.

I see_____

_____

_____

But I am outside,
looking inside

_____

I hear _____

_____

_____

But I am outside,
looking inside

_____

Kites

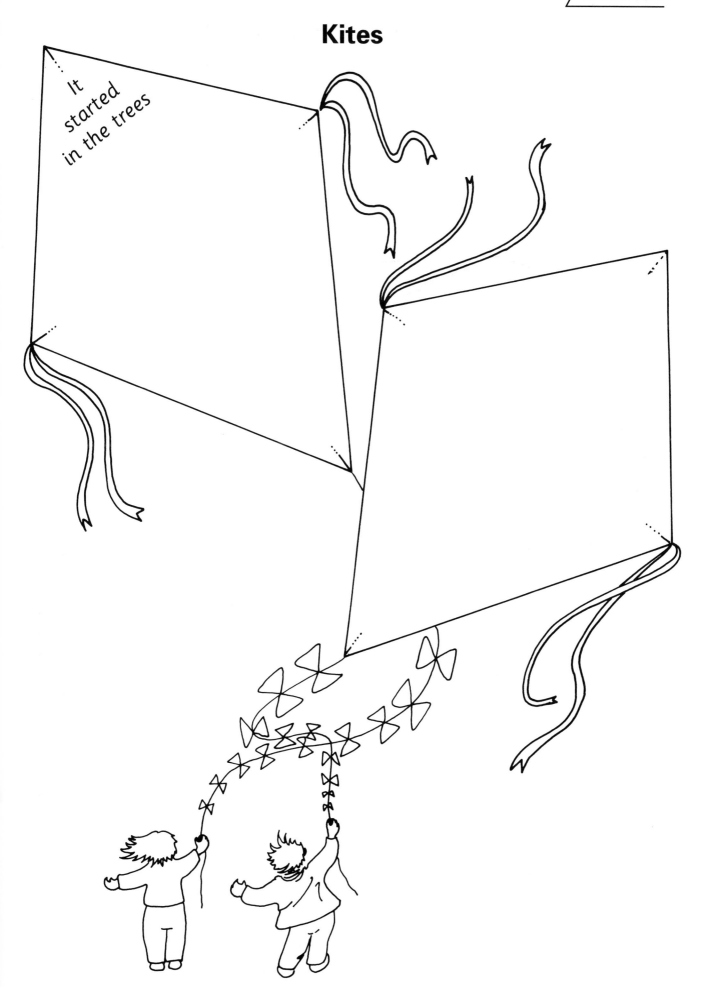

It started in the trees

The topic of the elements opens children's minds to perhaps some of the deepest thoughts they can have.

Copymaster 37 (Who lives here?)

A This copymaster presents children with a simple pattern poem to complete. Encourage the children to think of a creature of the earth and of the air for the second and fourth verses. For the third verse suggest something that moves within the fire – a spark, flame or smoke. The movement words are most important and three are required for each verse.

Ask the children to suggest words orally, but the teacher should write down just two ideas for each verse. From this, the children can draft on the 'borrow one, find two' principle, so that those who find it difficult have something concrete to work on. (Children 'borrow' one idea from the board and find another two of their own.)

Display the finished poem in a concertina format, with a verse and an illustration to each fold.

B Follow up this poem by looking at different kinds of homes, for example a castle, cottage or trailer, and using the same pattern.

C Invent more question and answer poems. For example:

What does the magic mirror hold?
'My shadow,' said the ghost.
'I shake and scare and flap
in the corner of the castle.'

What does the magic mirror hold?
'My reflection,' said the fairy godmother.
'I ...
in ...'

Copymaster 38 (What am I?)

A Read the poem 'Power' in the Anthology on page 80. Each two lines hides a letter of the alphabet. (The first letter is F, L, A, M or E, not S, P, A, R or K). Put together, the hidden letters spell the element described in the last four lines (FIRE).

Let the children make up a riddle in the same way for another of the elements, using the copymaster to help. First, brainstorm earth/air/water words. Look for images of colour, movement, touch and so on. For example:

Water looks like *a blue ribbon, a silver snake*
Water moves like *an eagle swooping, a horse galloping*
Water feels like *smooth silk, an icy cloak*
Water sounds like *a lion roaring, a child whispering*

Ask children to choose two looking-like, moving-like, feeling-like and sounding-like ideas for themselves,

borrowing one and finding one. The children should assemble these ideas in list form and then write a riddle in the first person, asking a question at the end. The children should complete the water riddle on the copymaster before writing their own. The completed water riddle could look like this:

I look like a blue ribbon
waving in the summer breeze.
I move like an eagle
swooping across the rocks.
I feel like an icy cloak
wrapping your shoulders.
I sound like a child
whispering in the dark.

What am I?

B Make one-poem books to display the riddles. Fold an A4 sheet as shown below, and write or draw the answer beneath it.

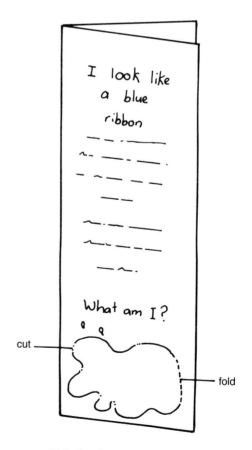

Open-poem riddle book

C Link the poetry of the elements to work in technology and science.

Copymaster 39 (Dress the elements)

[A] For this magical poem the children should explore each element in terms of colour and shape. Link these ideas with clothes. Look at the fashion pages of the newspaper. Suggest that each individual or group is a fashion designer to the elements and should design an appropriate garment for each element in words and pictures, filling in the spaces on the copymaster. Use colour and texture.

[B] Use the same idea for poems to dress a mountain, the seashore and a forest for summer/winter. Illustrate the finished poem in colour.

Copymaster 40 (Underground poem)

[A] This copymaster provides a frame for underground poems. Cut out the centre of the copymaster to make an overlay for a finished poem or cut the centre partially to make a door that opens to reveal a poem placed underneath it.

To write the poem itself, start by brainstorming underground words and ideas, for example 'darkness', 'dankness', 'mystery', 'treasure', 'fear', 'spookiness' and so on. Build the ideas into a short poem – perhaps a haiku, an acrostic or a cinquain.

[B] Another idea is to ask questions in the poem, for example 'What secret lies at the end of the tunnel?' or 'What's behind the mystery door?' The poem can be written on the centre of the copymaster, cut as described above to make a door. The solution to the mystery can then be placed underneath the door. Other poems could be written along the same lines, each with a flap to conceal the answer. For example, 'What's inside the treasure chest?', 'What's at the bottom of the wishing well?' and 'What lies behind the castle door?'

AIR

FIRE

Power

My first is in flame,
but not in spark,
my second in light,
not in the dark.
My third is in flicker,
but not in night,
my last in candle,
but not in bright.
My whole is orange
and yellow and red,
without me, the world
would long be dead.

What am I?

Moira Andrew

Water moods

picking	retrieving
up	a
and	sodden
squeezing	grey
the	tennis-ball
sponge-ball	dropped
in	in
the	a
bath	November
is	puddle
pure	is
pleasure	not

Gary Boswell

EARTH

WATER

Who lives here?

Who lives in water?
'I do,' said the fish.
'I swim and dance and dive
in clean clear water.'

Who lives in the air?

'I do,' said the _____

_____

_____

Who lives in fire?

'I do,' said the _____

_____

_____

Who lives in the earth?

'I do,' said the _____

_____

_____

Complete the poem in your own words, using the first verse as a
pattern. Make a concertina book and write one verse on each page.

　　　　　　　　　　　　　　　　Copymaster 37

What am I?

'Power' is a riddle hiding one of the four elements. Can you guess what it is?

To write a riddle of your own, choose a different element. Suggest ideas to describe colour, movement, touch and sound:

what it looks like _____

how it moves _____

what it feels like_____

what it sounds like _____

Ask a question at the end.

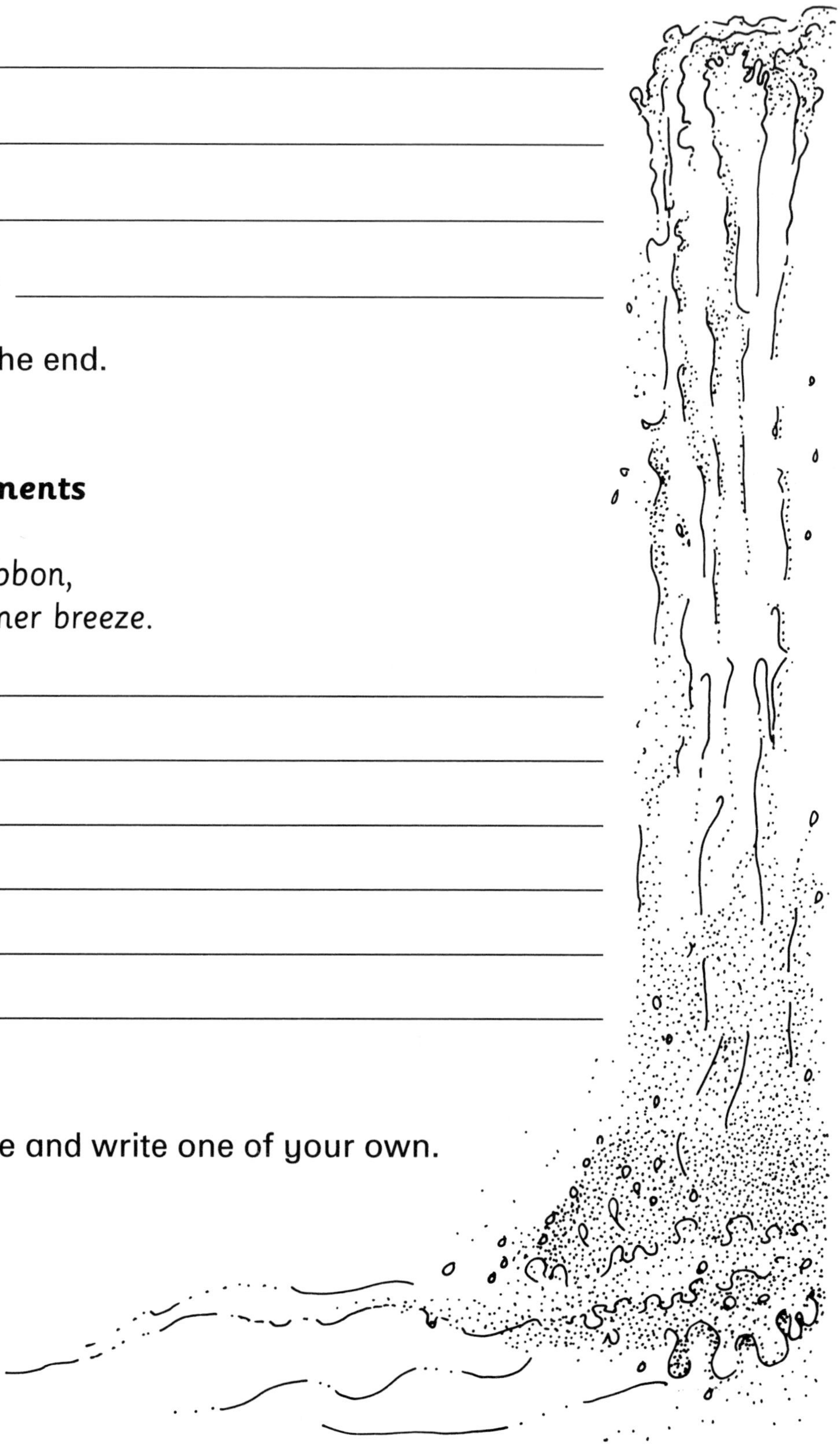

Riddle of the elements

I look like a blue ribbon,
waving in the summer breeze.

I move like _____

_____

I feel like _____

_____

I sound like _____

_____

What am I?

Finish off this riddle and write one of your own.

Copymaster 38

Dress the elements

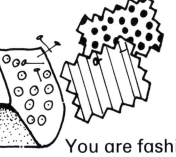

You are fashion editor to the elements!
Design fabulous outfits to make the most
of each element.

For the air around us
cut out an invisible cloak
studded with sequins
made from drops of
morning dew

For clear bright water

For the heat of fire

For the deep brown earth

Illustrate your designs in colour.

Copymaster 39

Underground poem

MYTHICAL BEASTS

The topic on mythical beasts encourages children to unlock their imaginations in a way that work on real animals does not. They can indulge in flights of fancy, design creatures that could never exist, paint them in all the colours of the rainbow – and who is to say they are wrong? None of us has ever seen a dragon, so anything goes!

Copymaster 41 (Dizzy dragon)

A This copymaster is based on alliteration and will appeal to the children's sense of humour. Those who are not turned on by more traditional descriptive pieces often enjoy exploring the fun of this approach.

Read the 'Dizzy dragon' poem on the copymaster and find endings to fit. Can the children work out what is needed? Indicate how alliteration works.

The copymaster also has more poem starters along the same lines. Ask individuals or groups to work on the 'Terrible troll' and 'Miserable monster' poems. (You might award a small prize or a medal made from card on a pin for the funniest or cleverest poem.) Encourage the children to be quite zany in their ideas. They should illustrate the poems when they've finished, putting the words inside speech bubbles, and collect them together in a class comic book.

Make up more 'Crazy creature' poems.

B Use alliteration to make up poems about 'Potty people', 'Trendy teachers', 'Nosy neighbours', 'Peppery poets', 'Modern mums' and so on.

Copymaster 42 (Recipe for a unicorn)

A Read the poem 'Recipe for a unicorn' in the Anthology on page 87. Talk about the special way it is written using recipe instructions.

Use an illustrated book of mythical creatures. Look for unicorns, dragons and mermaids. Talk about the special characteristics of each, for example the unicorn's single spiral horn, fine long mane, white coat and delicate hooves.

Encourage the children to think of way-out imaginative ideas to find things in nature which best suggest parts of the creature's body, for example a waterfall for the unicorn's mane, silver stars for the hooves and newly-fallen snow for its white coat.

As a class or individual activity choose another mythical creature, draw a picture of it on the copymaster and show with arrows what makes it special. Encourage the children to brainstorm fantastic magical ideas from nature to suggest the shape or colour of each part of their creature's body, making a 'shopping list' of ideas.

Putting the 'shopping list' to one side, talk about the recipe form and the use of cookbook words such as 'take', 'add', 'mix' and so on. Now the poem can be put together like a magic recipe. Encourage the children to use the ideas they themselves have suggested, crossing out each phrase on the 'shopping list' as it is used in the poem. Make a cookbook for each recipe, with one verse and accompanying illustration on each page.

A mythical beast cookbook

B Move on to thinking and writing about less familiar mythical creatures, for example griffins, cyclops and hobbits. Use a similar format to the unicorn poem. While this task frees the imagination and encourages children to think in metaphorical terms, the recipe structure provides a framework within which to write.

C Use a recipe format to work on poems about the seasons, for example spring:

Take some delicate snowdrops,
primroses shining like stars
and a morning of pale sunshine.

Add ...

and so on, making up several three-line verses, finishing
with the valedictory line 'And you have made SPRING!'

Copymaster 43 (If I had lived in days of old)

A Get children to look in the library for books on
myths and legends, and read 'Dragon days' in the
Anthology on page 87. Working in pairs, children
should list the things they have missed out on because
they live *now*, not in 'days of old'.

The children should write a poem, beginning with
one of the two starting lines on the copymaster and,
from their list, suggesting some of the exciting or
magical things that don't happen any more – if indeed
they ever did! The children need to find rhyming words
for this piece of work to make it as much fun as possible.
The copymaster can be stuck on backing paper, with the
castle door cut out as a flap. The finished poem can then
be written on the backing paper under the door.

B In contrast, children can suggest a list of things
they would have missed if they had lived in days of old –
TV, cars, computer games, central heating and so on. A
poem of the present can then be written to match the
olden days poem. This can be displayed inside a
computer-screen outline.

Copymaster 44 (Monster find)

A Let children read the newspaper article on the
copymaster about the unknown monster. Ask the
children to try building up a picture of the monster in
their mind's eye. Suggest that they think of size, shape
and special characteristics, all inferred from the clues in
the article. Some may wish to draw the monster.

This piece of work will be a 'found poem', that is, it
uses some of the words already on the copymaster
together with some of the children's own phrases to fill
it out. It makes it easier for the children if the article is
first photocopied, so that they can physically cut it up
into lines. They should discard the bits they don't want
and add their own descriptions, trying to give the
finished poem a rhythm.

The poem might look a bit like this (words in italics
are from the article on the copymaster):

Mystery monster

Enormous as *a blue whale*,
the monster swam and paddled
through dark prehistoric seas.

When it walked on land,
the creature *stood tall*, making
giant footsteps in the mud.

With its *long hairy coat*,
eyes as round as stones,
and *teeth* as *sharp* as knives,

this mystery monster
leaves question marks
across the pages of history.

Although the poem uses many of the original words
and ideas, it has totally changed the character of the
writing.

B Look for other newspaper articles, recipes or prose
pieces that can be used as the basis of a 'found poem'.
The instructions on the backs of seed packets make
good poems cut up and added to in this way.

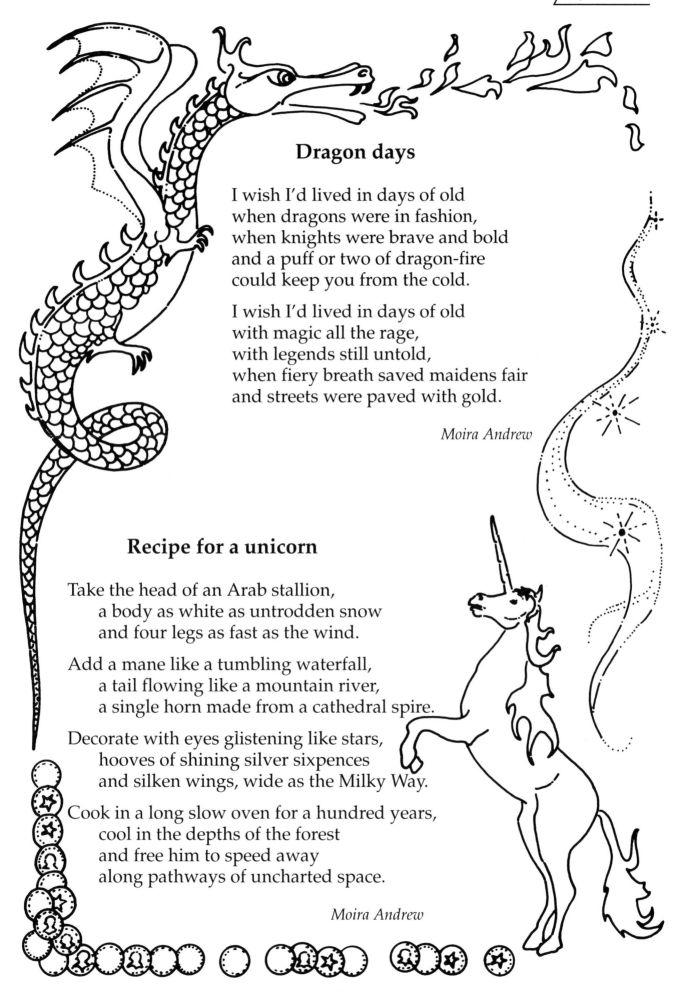

Dragon days

I wish I'd lived in days of old
when dragons were in fashion,
when knights were brave and bold
and a puff or two of dragon-fire
could keep you from the cold.

I wish I'd lived in days of old
with magic all the rage,
with legends still untold,
when fiery breath saved maidens fair
and streets were paved with gold.

Moira Andrew

Recipe for a unicorn

Take the head of an Arab stallion,
    a body as white as untrodden snow
    and four legs as fast as the wind.

Add a mane like a tumbling waterfall,
    a tail flowing like a mountain river,
    a single horn made from a cathedral spire.

Decorate with eyes glistening like stars,
    hooves of shining silver sixpences
    and silken wings, wide as the Milky Way.

Cook in a long slow oven for a hundred years,
    cool in the depths of the forest
    and free him to speed away
    along pathways of uncharted space.

Moira Andrew

Dizzy dragon

I'm a dizzy dragon
who delights in daffodil drinks,
who drums on dusty doorbells

who draws with _____

who dreams of _____

Yes, I'm a dizzy dragon
who doesn't know
        night from day!

I'm a terrible troll

who _____

I'm a miserable monster

who _____

Can you make up more silly poems like this about ugly unicorns,
musical mermaids, jolly giants and other crazy creatures?

Copymaster 41

Recipe for a unicorn

Mythical beasts are fabulous creatures of the imagination. Draw one in colour and show with arrows what makes it special.

Now look for something from nature which has the shape or colour to fit in with the special parts of your creature.

Read 'Recipe for a unicorn' and put a recipe poem together in the same way. Let your imagination go to town!

Recipe for _____

Take _____

and _____

Add _____

and _____

Decorate with _____

and _____

Cook for _____

and you have made a _____

Copymaster 42

If I had lived in days of old

Begin a poem with either:

If I had lived in days of old

or

I wish I'd lived in days of old

Copymaster 43

Monster find

Scientists have unearthed the bones of a previously unknown monster. The living creature would have weighed about 300kg and must have been about the size of a blue whale.

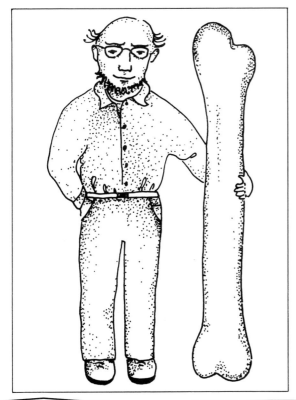

The monster could swim, but scientists believe that it could also walk on land. When it swam, 50 million years ago, it probably used its legs like flippers. When it walked, it stood tall and almost certainly took giant rolling footsteps.

There is some doubt about what the monster looked like, although it is known that it had a long hairy coat, great sharp teeth and eyes as round as stones. The big questions are: Where did it sleep? What did it eat? Who were its enemies? And how did it look?

Cut this newspaper article into lines. Arrange the lines and add words of your own to make a poem describing the monster.
Answer the questions that baffled the scientists.

To make your poem look different, draw a monster shape and write the poem around it.

PORTRAITS

Encourage the children to think of portraits in poetry as being like painted portraits, using words instead of paint. When writing about people, children should be helped to look not simply at appearance, but at the attributes that make that person who he or she is. Ask questions about the people in profile: What do you like about them? What annoys you about them? What do they do or say that makes you laugh? What funny habits or peculiarities do they have?

Encourage children to listen to the person they are going to write about. Does he or she have any pet phrases? Children could tell a story about something they have done that is typical of that person.

Copymaster 45 (If I were an artist)

A Tell the children that they can design a personalised dinosaur, completing the poem on the copymaster. They can decide where he lives, how he sounds, what he likes to eat. Ask the children to think of the dinosaur's shape and size, and the colours they would paint him.

Suggest that the dinosaur should be quite fabulous – rainbow-patterned scales, perhaps, spikes pointed like pyramids, a voice like a thunderstorm. Encourage the children to look for way-out comparisons from the natural world. Talk about the range of possibilities before the children begin work on the copymaster.

Everyone should use the same opening lines:

> If I were an artist
> I'd paint the portrait
> of a dinosaur.

Work on more three-line verses beginning with parts of the dinosaur's body: back, head, tail, eyes, teeth, claws, spikes and so on. For example:

> For his scales,
> I'd use all the colours
> of the rainbow.

Encourage each child to finish his or her poem in their own way, then draw and colour the dinosaur, paying particular attention to the details described in the poem.

B Now get children to design a griffin, a troll or a mermaid, and paint its portrait in words, drawing and colouring a fabulous creature to match the poem.

C Using a similar format, children could paint a portrait of the headteacher, Grandma, a favourite uncle or the next-door neighbour in words.

D Word-portraits of someone known to everyone in the class (from school or from TV) could be exchanged, the reader guessing who is being described.

E Display the portraits inside decorated card or paper frames, as shown below. Hang all the framed portraits together to make a gallery.

  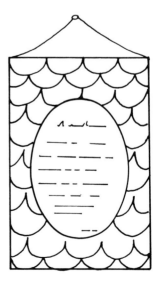

A word-portrait gallery

Copymaster 46 (Mirror, mirror on the wall)

A Bring a distorting mirror, for example a shaving mirror, into class. Speculate on what might happen if it were a magic mirror with a tale to tell. If it was really ancient, what faces of history might have passed before it? Build up a background to the mirror, then brainstorm ideas about it on the board.

Children should imagine the face that is peering into the magic mirror. If the mirror could speak, what questions would it ask? (Children might like to work in pairs for this task.) The three questions on the copymaster should be answered, then another five thought of. The blanks on the copymaster should be filled in, so that there are eight questions and eight answers, the zanier the better!

The answers should be used to make an eight-line portrait poem of the ghostly character whose face appears in the magic mirror. Children can make a faint pencil crayon drawing of the face inside the mirror frame and write out the poem on top.

B Use an old black and white or sepia photograph of a First World War soldier, a Red Cross nurse, a Second World War airman, Grandma or Grandad as a child. With the class imagine asking questions of the face in the photograph. Children write down the questions they would like to ask and invent answers. A portrait poem can be made from the answers. Frame the poem with a black and white pen-and-ink pattern.

C Use the same photograph for a descriptive piece of writing about the person in the picture.

Copymaster 47 (Portrait of Grandma)

A Read the poem 'My Gran' from the Anthology on page 94. It is a growing poem which describes Grandma by some of the things she used to say and do. All the descriptive words are joined by hyphens in this poem to give it a pattern on the page and to help the rhythm along.

On the copymaster the children make up a poem about someone they know well – their grandma, grandad, brother, sister, aunt or uncle – using this pattern. They gather together a list of some of the things these people say and do which, in the children's eyes, make them who they are. Children should put a hyphen between each word and listen to the rhythm of each phrase. There is space on the copymaster for children to draw a portrait of the person in question.

The children add an extra line to each verse until they have used up all their ideas. Their poem doesn't have to rhyme.

B The children think of some of the things they say every day. They think of the things they like doing best and the things they absolutely hate! The children list them and add hyphens to make the rhythms work using 'My Gran' as a pattern. The finished poems are put anonymously into a folder. The children can ask their friends to draw out a poem and guess whose portrait it is.

Copymaster 48 (Things they say)

A Talk about different 'nagging' people – parents, brothers and sisters, traffic wardens, teachers! The children write down these people's most over-used phrases and use their ideas to write a portrait poem on the copymaster.

Develop the poem into a performance piece, perhaps using costumes, hats or other props.

B Follow up with a 'reply' poem in which the nagged person answers back! Talk about the all-too-familiar nags: 'How many times have I told you?' 'When are you going to learn?' 'I'm fed up telling you …' and so on. (Find out the most commonly used nags and show them on a graph.) Build the nags up into a dialogue poem.

My Gran

My Gran is
    a giggle-in-the-corner-like-a-child
        kind of Gran

She is
    a put-your-cold-hand-in-my-pocket
    a keep-your-baby-curls-in-my-locket
        kind of Gran

She is
    a make-it-better-with-a-treacle-toffee
    a what-you-need's-a-cup-of-milky-coffee
    a hurry-home-I-love-you-awfully
        kind of Gran

She is
    a butter-ball-for-your-bad-throat
    a stitch-your-doll-a-new-green-coat
    a let's-make-soapy-bubbles-float
    a hold-my-hand-I'm-seasick-in-a-boat
        kind of Gran

She is
    a toast-your-tootsies-by-the-fire
    a crack-the-wishbone-for-your-heart's-desire
    a ladies-don't-sweat-they-perspire
    a slow-to-burn-occasionally-furious-spitfire
    a funny-old-fashioned-higgledy-piggledy-lady-to-admire
        kind of Gran

And this lovely grandmother
    is mine, all mine!

Moira Andrew

Song for an enemy

If I were the rain I'd wait till you come out,
Then drip, plop! right on your head.

If I were a shoe I'd tickle your feet when you put me on.

If I were the snow I would pile up above your door
Then woosh! slide down your neck.

If I were your pillow I'd be hard and lumpy.

If I were the wind, I would sing you to sleep,
Then wake you up with a roar!

David Orme

If I were an artist

Design your own *personal* dinosaur. Make it quite fabulous.

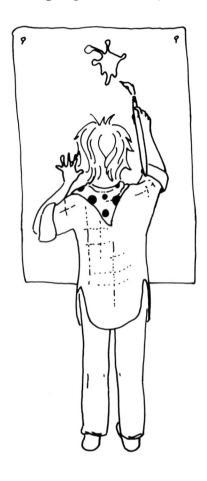

If I were an artist,
I'd paint the portrait
of a dinosaur.

For its scales ...

For its back ...

For its head ...

For its tail ...

For its eyes ...

For its teeth ...

Draw and colour your dinosaur.

Copymaster 45

Mirror, mirror on the wall

This is a magic mirror with a tale to tell. If it could speak, what questions would it ask?

- Who are you?

- Where do you come from?

- Are you dead or alive?

-

-

-

-

-

Make a list of questions and answers, the more zany the better!

Write out each answer on a separate line to make a portrait poem of this zany character. Make a faint pencil-crayon drawing of your character inside the mirror outline and write the poem on top.

Copymaster 46

Portrait of Grandma

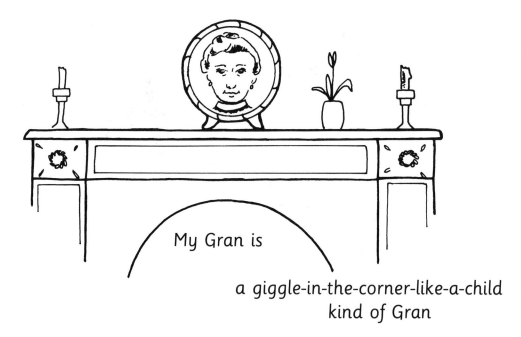

My Gran is

a giggle-in-the-corner-like-a-child
kind of Gran

Make up a poem about *your* Grandma or Grandad, brother or sister, aunt or uncle using this pattern. Draw their portrait in the empty frame.

'My Gran' rhymes, but your poem doesn't have to.

Copymaster 47

Things they say

Here are some of the things they say,
Nag! nag! nag! every day!

   Tidy your bedroom!
   Pick up your toys!
   Take your elbows off the table!

Here are some of the things they say,
Nag! nag! nag! every day!

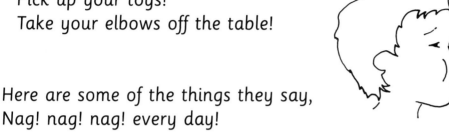

_____

_____

_____

Here are some of the things they say,
Nag! nag! nag! every day!

_____

_____

_____

Those are some of the things they say
Sometimes I wish they would go away!

Copymaster 48

THE SEA

The sea is a perennial topic, offering great variety in colour, sound and mood. Encourage the children to think of the sea, not simply in terms of holidays, but in its wild and dangerous moods. Think of the variety of creatures for whom the sea is home, of the sea as a source of food, of the sea as history, of the contrast between the surface and the depths, of the sea as a 'magic carpet' stretching from one country to another.

Copymaster 49 (Sea through the senses)

A This poem works best if the children have been on a visit to the seaside. Failing that, use pictures, posters, music and children's holiday memories.

Encourage the children to look and listen, to touch – even to smell and taste. Each verse of the poem will begin with one of the senses: 'Look at the sea', 'Listen to the sea' and so on.

Now brainstorm words to describe the sea. Ask children to choose four words that particularly appeal to them, for example 'blue', 'sparkling', 'deep' and 'cold'. String the adjectives together, using a different order each time and use them as part of the second and third lines:

> Look at the sea,
> sparkling, blue and cold,
> deep as ...
>
> ...
>
> Listen to the sea,
> blue and cold and deep,
> sparkling ...
>
> ...

Encourage each child to look for a different ending, for example:

> deep as an endless
> mine shaft.
>
> deep as the ends
> of the earth.
>
> deep as the farthest
> edge of space.

Fill in the copymaster with five verses altogether, all written to the same pattern.

B Use the same idea for writing about the wind, snow and rain.

Copymaster 50 (Underwater world)

A This copymaster is based on acrostics. The acrostic poem can be read downwards as well as across, the initial letters of each line making up the title of the poem.

The children should finish the UNDERWATER WORLD acrostic which has been started on the copymaster. Try DOLPHIN, then look at the picture and choose another creature to write about, beginning by writing the title in capital letters, downwards on the page. The trick is to make sure that each line tells something more about the sea creature, and the poem as a whole describes it in some detail. Many children see these acrostics as something of a puzzle to be solved and enjoy the challenge it sets.

B Write acrostic poems about children in the group, using their names as initial letters for each line.

C Write acrostics for the seasons, the town/village/city where you live, the place where children are going on holiday.

D Find a suitable picture and let children write acrostics based on what they see in it. Glue the finished acrostics, like mini-poems, on appropriate places on the picture (see below) or make them into a frame to surround it.

An acrostic display

Copymaster 51 (Sea sounds)

[A] This copymaster is an exercise in alliteration. Perform 'Beach music' on the copymaster with the class a number of times. Make it into a piece of choral speaking, either in unison or as a round. Then start the class off on 'Storm music' which they should complete, finding words and consonants to suggest the sound of a storm.

[B] When the children have worked on their poems and are confident enough to perform them, add percussion or use any classical piece of sea music as an accompaniment, set behind the words. Try *Fingal's Cave* and make up poems to reflect the sound of the sea in all its different moods.

[C] There are many other possibilities for alliterative poems along these lines – 'Rain music', 'Traffic music' and 'Train music' for example.

Copymaster 52 (Sea haiku)

[A] Haiku are brief poems, Japanese in origin, with a 5–7–5 syllable pattern. Ensure that the children are confident in their understanding of syllables before they start. A good way into syllable counting is to use the children's own first names: Ben, John, Clare (one-syllable names); Katy, Michael, Hayley (two-syllable names); Christopher, Jonathon, Melissa (three-syllable names); Victoria, Alexander, Elizabeth (four-syllable names).

Because Haiku are so short, they are best used for single observations, especially ones with an element of surprise or contrast – a granite rock unmoving against a crashing wave, bright-red holly berries against pure, white snow. Use the copymaster to write sea haiku. Encourage children to draft their ideas first, then to shape them into haiku, rather than launching into the exercise straight away. Children should use the words they think they need, then refine them to fit into the syllable count.

[B] Once the haiku form is understood, it can be used for any of the topics in this book, given the strengths and limitations mentioned above. Other syllable poems include the cinquain (see page 122).

[C] When the haiku is mastered, children can be encouraged to write a set of three to five of them on a single topic. This is called a renga. Use the renga as mini-poems pasted around a relevant scene: for a sea renga, the scene could include harbour, gulls, fishing boats, yachts, buoys, lifeboat and so on.

Sea song

Splash of fish
and dart of fin,
crustacean scuttles
out and in.

Sway of frond
and flash of scale,
glimpse of silver,
flick of tail.

Shark-like shadows
gliding near:
now it's time
to disappear.

Tony Mitton

Sea seasons

The sea bounces
over barnacles,
bobbing and buckling
in the springtime breeze.

The sea slithers
across shingle,
splintering and sparkling
under a bright summer sun.

The sea prowls
over pebbles,
pimpling and prickling
on damp autumn days.

The sea rushes
across rocks,
ranting and raving
when winter winds blow.

Moira Andrew

Sea through the senses

Take four words to describe the sea, for example 'blue', 'sparkling', 'deep' and 'cold'. String them together, using a different order each time, and use one of the senses to start each line.

The first verse could look like this.

> Look at the sea,
> sparkling, blue and cold,
> deep as the bottom
> of the world.

Now complete the poem below using the words you chose.

Look at the sea,

_____

_____

_____

Listen to the sea,

_____

_____

_____

Touch the sea,

_____

_____

_____

Taste the sea,

_____

_____

_____

Smell the sea,

_____

_____

_____

Copymaster 49

Underwater world

Can you read 'UNDERWATER' in this acrostic poem? Make a new acrostic to fit the word 'WORLD'.

Under the waves
Nine fathoms deep
Derelict ships lie
Empty of life
Rocking to and fro
With the tides
And only the wind
Tells of the lonely wrecks
Ever-swaying to the
Rhythms of the sea.

W _____

O _____

R _____

L _____

D _____

Now complete the poem below.

D _____

O _____

L _____

P _____

H _____

I _____

N _____

Make more acrostic poems from this underwater picture.

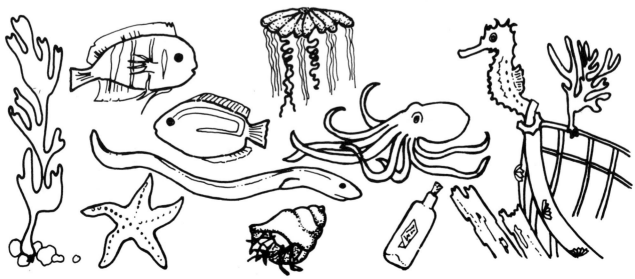

Copymaster 50

Sea sounds

Beach music

Ssh ... Ssh ... Ssh ...
listen to the surf,
slapping and sucking and rushing
on soft, sunlit days:
hear
the hiss and sizzle of foam
soaking into wet sand;
listen!
Ssh ... Ssh ... Ssh ...

Storm music

Crash! crash! crash!
Listen to

Copymaster 51

Sea haiku

With the rest of the class talk about the special haiku pattern and look at the example below.

> *See the greedy waves*
> *Gobble up rocks like ripe plums*
> *Then spit out the stones.*

Complete the sea haiku below.

(5)   An old rusty ship

(7)

(5)

Now write your own sea haiku.

(5)

(7)

(5)

Copymaster 52

SENSES

Poems which have a direct link to the senses often turn out to produce very sensitive writing and can be a pathway into the emotions.

Copymaster 53 (Taste of autumn)

A This copymaster turns the usual senses back to front. Children should look outside and think of the changes autumn brings, then draw pictures in the spaces on the copymaster. They then write a single sentence under each drawing.

Ask the children to think about the smell of autumn (bonfires, mist, chestnuts), the colours of autumn, autumn seeds, falling leaves, animals getting ready for winter. Now let children imagine if all these things had a *taste*. What might they taste like?

Look at the first verse printed on the copymaster and ask the children to complete it from one of the sentences they have suggested. Then move on to other places where autumn could be tasted. Use posters and music to help the flow of ideas.

Remind the children that they should not try to make these poems rhyme. By all means, they can listen to the beat, but struggling for a suitable rhyme often up-ends all the sensitive writing they have tried to put together.

B Make up more verses: on the mountain, in the garden, in the playground.

C Use another of the senses and write similar poems, beginning: 'Hear autumn in the trees' or 'Touch autumn in misty mornings'.

D Use this pattern to write poems about spring, summer and winter.

E Display the round-the-year poems on a circle divided into four segments: spring on green backing paper, summer on yellow, autumn on orange and winter on pale blue.

Copymaster 54 (Colour poems)

A This copymaster again begins with list-making. Encourage the children to think of things in nature which are *always* green – not the lamp-post outside the school which just happens to be painted green!

Children fill in the list first, then read 'What is green?' from the Anthology on page 108, looking at the pattern the poet has used:

Deep-down, the sea is green

In the same way, if the children want to begin with the idea of leaves they might begin:

On high, new leaves are green

and so on. Help the children to find a double-beat description to begin each second line, as in 'What is green?'

B Use the same pattern to work on poems about different colours, helping the children to look for things in nature which are *always* white or blue or red.

C Display the finished poems on a rainbow shape cut out and pinned across the corner of the classroom wall. Let the poems hang from the 'rainbow' inside a border of the appropriate colour. Place them inside a circle or a raindrop shape.

Copymaster 55 (Haunted house)

A This is a listening poem which tells the story of a visit to a haunted house through sounds only. The children should think of more ghostly sounds to finish the poem. These need not be real words – the children can invent new words that sound right.

B Let the children think of other noisy environments: a busy street, a classroom, a factory, a forest in a storm. They should tell the story of these places in sound only. Stress that the poem should not simply be a list of appropriate noises, but should tell a story in sound.

Working in groups, each group asks the others to guess what is happening in their story-poem by listening to the sounds they have created.

Copymaster 56 (Making sense)

This is a brainstorming sheet that can be used in several ways. Its primary purpose is to collect ideas for a sense poem.

A Children place a small object in the 'What am I?' box. Children use the columns to list sense words and phrases. These could be literal descriptions or similes.

B Children draw a picture of an object in the box, then use the columns in the same way.

C Children draw an object in the box, then stick a flap over the picture. A second child uses the words and phrases to guess what is under the flap.

A sense of season

I touched autumn today.
It sat in my hand, damp
and dank as a frog.

Today I saw autumn
light apple lanterns
on boughs sad with rain.

I tasted autumn today,
cool as mints dipped
in the sugar of winter.

Today I smelled autumn
in smoke curls unwinding
into dragon-misted air.

Today I listened
to autumn's lament
haunting the treetops.

Moira Andrew

What is green?

Deep-down, the sea is green,
    dark with sunken mysteries.
High-up, the hills are green,
    veiled beneath nets of cloud.

Sky-tall, forests are green,
    shadowed with dreams of night.
Grass-wide, meadows are green,
    fingered by morning mist.

Steam-moist, jungles are green,
    jewelled with birds of paradise.
Sunlit, rainforests are green,
    touched by the breath of hope.

Moira Andrew

Taste of autumn

Think of cool autumn days, of leaves changing colour and falling, of darker mornings, evenings drawing in.

Draw autumn pictures and write a sentence for each.

You have drawn what you can *see* as autumn comes along. Now imagine that you can *taste* autumn. Write a poem about autumn from your sentences, like this perhaps:

Taste autumn in the woods,
in the changing colours,
in the fallen leaves,

in the _____

Taste autumn on the seashore,

in the _____

_____

_____

Taste autumn by the river,

_____

_____

_____

Make up more verses: on the mountain, in the garden, in the playground.

Copymaster 53

Colour poems

List as many natural green things as you can.

- grass
- new leaves
- hills
-
-
-
-

-
-
-
-
-
-

Read the poem 'What is green?' from the Anthology. Make up a poem that uses the same pattern.

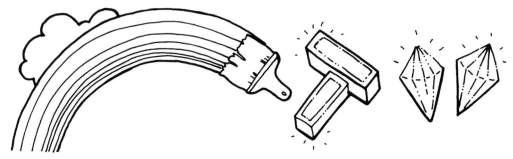

Think of all the blue things in nature: summer sea, bluebells, forget-me-nots and so on. List them and make up another 'What is?' colour poem.

Write a 'What is white?' poem.

Write a 'What is red?' poem.

Haunted house

This poem does not have proper words, just sounds! It tells the story of a visit to a haunted house.

Can you finish it?

Tip tap tip tap tip tap
CREAK!
Tip tap tip tap tip ...
THUD!
SCREECH!
Tiptaptiptaptiptap
Rattle rattle
CREAK
Bump
  Bump
    Bump
      Bump ...

111

Making sense

What am I?

I feel like

_____

_____

_____

_____

I taste like

_____

_____

_____

_____

I look like

_____

_____

_____

_____

I smell like

_____

_____

_____

_____

I sound like

_____

_____

_____

_____

Copymaster 56

SPACE

Space and space travel, astronauts and aliens all hold a tremendous fascination for primary-school children. Although often considered solely as a science topic, it can provide a range of imaginative and exciting writing activities.

Copymaster 57 (Poet in space)

A This copymaster gives children practice in using simile and metaphor, the basis of much descriptive poetry. Ask the group to think about the darkest places they know – under the stairs, inside the wardrobe, in an underground cave. Brainstorm words relating to colour, fear, mystery and so on – all connected with the idea of darkness.

Suggest to the children that they are travellers in space. They have to report back to NASA, but are unable to take photographs and must rely on the written word instead.

Work from the 'shopping list' of words collected in the brainstorming session, encouraging children towards the use of image. For example, 'Space is like an empty box', 'like the depths of the sea', 'like a war-torn church'. Let children fill in the lines on the copymaster to make a beginning to the poem, and then find more similes to complete it.

B Write poems in silver pen on black paper with words arranged in a spiral as suggested on the copymaster. Display the poems grouped on a space background of meteors, stars and planets, created by blowing paint through straws or by using oil-based pastel crayons.

C All the topics in this book can be used as a basis for image or simile poems.

Copymaster 58 (Nursery rhymes)

A This copymaster practises the use of rhythm and rhyme. Ask the children which nursery rhymes they remember or borrow a book of nursery rhymes from the reception class.

Read 'Star song' from the Anthology on page 116. Ask children which nursery rhyme it fits. Remind the children of 'Sing a song of sixpence'.

To complete the copymaster the children can work in pairs or groups. They have the first four lines of 'Star song'. Can they work together to make up new verses to finish off the poem, using space words and ideas? The children need to watch the rhyme and try to keep to the original rhythm. It doesn't matter if the nursery rhyme turns out to be a bit of a joke – this kind of poem doesn't have to make complete sense!

B Now choose a different first line, for example 'Sing a song of spaceships' or 'Sing a song of astronauts' and let children make up a new rhyme following the original pattern and keeping to the rhythm.

C Try the same idea using a different nursery rhyme.

D Now try fitting another topic ('Machines', 'The sea', 'Creatures') to a nursery rhyme pattern.

E Star names are attractive (Alpha Centauri, Betelgeuse, Sirius, Epsilon Eridani). Collect the names and turn them into a chant or a comic rhyming poem.

Copymaster 59 (Space mini-poems)

A Read the poem on the copymaster, in which the poet describes a comet as 'a wish with wings'. Look at the other space pictures on the copymaster with the class and think of how to describe the moon, a planet, the sun. Collect ideas, for example if the moon is like 'a silver boat' think of how a boat 'sails' or 'drifts' or 'tosses'.

Encourage the children to write their own poems in no more than five lines. The moon poem might begin with: 'The moon, sailing/drifting/tossing' and finish with 'like a silver boat'.

B Children should write the finished poems inside the space outlines. They can then be coloured, cut out and pasted on a black or purple background.

C Children could write more mini-poems on space about the Milky Way, the Great Bear, Orion and other constellations of stars.

D Another possibility is a mini-poem describing the earth, looking down from space. Children could show a rocket from which astronauts are space-walking and write the mini-poems in speech bubbles, one for each astronaut (see over).

E Make a display with poems for every planet in the solar system, exploring the science and mythology of each.

F Ask children to write a set of haiku (see page 101) on a space theme.

A display of space mini-poems

Copymaster 60 (Alien interview)

A Working in groups the children should be asked to write down on the copymaster questions they would like to ask an alien. On a separate piece of paper they can then write the alien's answers. (It is a good idea to get groups to swap ideas, so that they have to answer other groups' questions.) The questions might look like this:

> What do you eat?
> What planet do you live on?
> What does it look like?

Encourage the children to use their answers to develop a poem, writing the finished version on the copymaster. For example:

I'm the last of my race,
A sad and lonely creature
     lost in space.
My planet once had a name,
But I've forgotten it,
     to my shame.
I live on small creeping things
I find under bare stones;
     Soon I'll just be bones.

This poem rhymes, but the children's don't have to.

B An alternative is to write a question and answer poem as in 'First dog on the moon'. (See Anthology, page 115.)

First dog on the moon

'Hi there,
First Dog on the Moon.
How do you feel?'

'Like nothing on Earth.'

'Yes, but can you taste anything up there?'

'Bones so cold and dry
They bite my tongue.'

'That's great, First Dog on the Moon.
Now, what can you smell?'

'Fear of the things hiding
In hard shadows.'

'OK, OK, so what can you see?'

'Long dead forests,
broken windows
in empty streets,
Things,
Shadows.'

'So what are you going to do next,
First Dog on the Moon?'

'Sit and howl at the Earth.'

David Orme

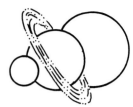

Star song

Sing a song of starshine,
twinkling from on high.
Four and twenty comets
whirling through the sky.

When the sky turns yellow
the stars put out their light
And whisper to the moonbeams
'We'll dance again tonight.'

Sing a song of starshine
travelling out in space,
Five and fifty mooncraft
revolving round the place.

When the doors are opened
the stars begin to sing.
Isn't that the coolest way to
announce the moon landing!

Sing a song of starshine
lighting up the dark.
Half a hundred space years
between us and each spark.

When the clever astronauts
arrive back from the moon,
They say, 'Wish we'd had a secret tape
to record each stellar tune!'

Moira Andrew

Poet in space

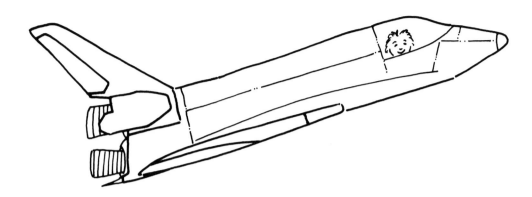

You are a traveller in space. Your camera is broken so NASA ask you, the poet, to describe space instead. Use similes in your poem.

Space is like _____

It is as dark as _____

It is as silent as _____

It is as mysterious as _____

For maximum effect write your poem in silver pen on black paper and arrange the words in a spiral.

　　　　　　　　　　　Copymaster 57

Nursery rhymes

Do you remember 'Sing a song of sixpence'?
Here is a new version using space words.

Sing a song of starshine,
twinkling from on high.
Four and twenty comets
whirling through the sky.

Make up more verses to finish off this poem. Watch the rhyme and try to keep the rhythm. Don't worry if it turns out to be a bit of a joke.

Now try and finish off the poems below:

Sing a song of spaceships,

_____

Four and twenty _____

_____

Or   Sing a song of spacemen,

Or   Sing a song of _____

Copymaster 58

Space mini-poems

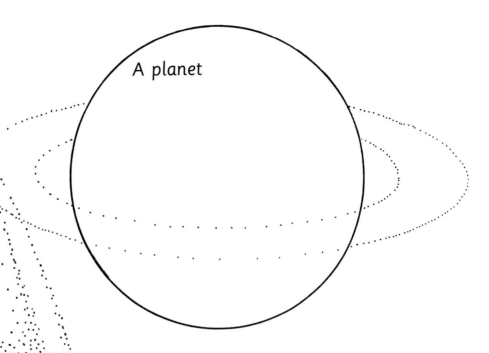

A planet

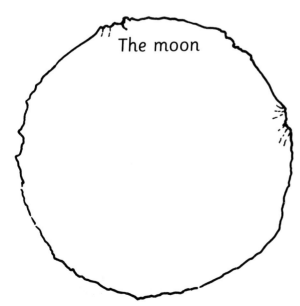

A comet, trailing
ribbons of stars,
careers across
the night sky like
a wish with wings.

Moira Andrew

The sun

The moon

119

Alien interview

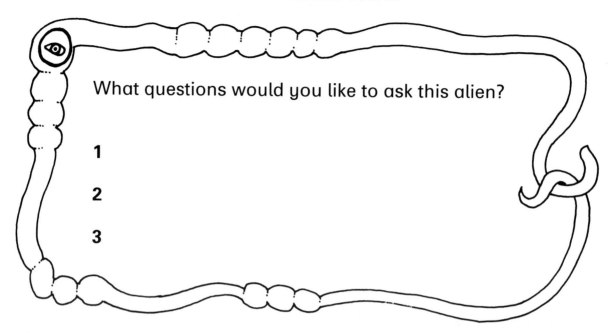

What questions would you like to ask this alien?

1

2

3

Your alien poem

Copymaster 60

Trees hold interest for children throughout the year. Trees, in parks and gardens, in playgrounds and on pavements, are part of every environment, in villages and towns alike, and children enjoy watching for the changes each season brings.

Copymaster 61 (Imagine a world without trees)

A Look at trees around the neighbourhood. Use a tree book and list the names of the trees within walking distance of school. Talk about the difference between evergreen and deciduous trees. Talk about the colour changes in deciduous leaves. Make a colour chart.

Ask children to think about the animals and birds who make their homes in and around trees, and find out what trees are used for when they are cut down.

Now the children should try to think what would be lost if the world had no trees left. Ask children to fill in the spaces on the copymaster, then put these ideas together to make a list poem.

Encourage the children to read their work aloud so that their words develop a rhythm. They should then divide the finished poem into verses and make up a chorus to go at the end of each verse. This should have a sad and lonely sound about it. Get the children to think of ways of putting sadness into words.

B To display the finished poem, use two sheets of A4 with the poem written out on the top sheet. Cut into a tree shape. Now make flaps with a 'no entry' road sign drawn on them as shown below. Cut them open, leaving a hinge, and underneath draw some of the things we would miss in a world without trees.

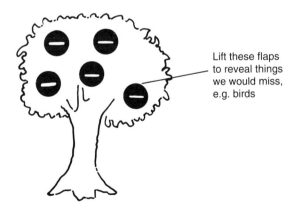

Lift these flaps to reveal things we would miss, e.g. birds

Copymaster 62 (Tree mini-poems)

A Use the artwork on the copymaster or ask the children to sketch a tree outline in pencil, preferably working directly from nature. Look at the shape, the texture of the bark, the roots, and any vegetation round the base of the tree. Make notes for mini-poems based on images: what the topmost branches look like ('a

ship's mast'?), how the birds move as they fly ('like children playing tag'?), how the birds perch ('like music notes'?) and so on down to the nettles, ferns and brambles at the foot of the tree.

Back in the classroom, the notes can be made into image mini-poems. Trace the tree outline (enlarged if necessary) in black ink on white paper and add the mini-poems, gluing them into place around the tree.

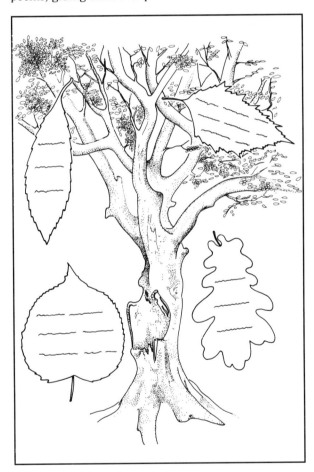

Tree mini-poems display

B A similar technique of writing haiku or mini-poems can be used with other settings, placing them in appropriate places around a pen and ink drawing of a castle, a plan of a nature walk, the seashore and so on. This helps those who are diffident about tackling a long descriptive poem and can be used as a group exercise.

Copymaster 63 (Tree songs)

A If you can, take the children on a day's outing to a forest or a woodland trail, and suggest that they *listen* to a tree. Children should find a tree, wrap their arms round it, put their ears against the trunk and listen. They can also listen to the sound of the wind in the

121

branches, the rain on the leaves, dry leaves crackling underfoot or branches snapping, or to the sound of birds, animals or water in the stream. Make a collection of forest sound words.

As a class or individual exercise use your tree books to identify as many different trees as you can. Write down the names.

Back in the classroom, ask children to choose a tree to draw in the space on the copymaster. They should now use some of the sound words and phrases collected to build up a song of the trees, completing the poem on the copymaster. The first two lines use a question and answer format. Children should follow this structure to complete the song with a different tree every time.

B Perform the finished song, as a class or group, as a piece for choral speaking. Add a chorus for everybody to say together, so they sound like the whole forest speaking.

C Use percussion instruments to add an accompaniment to the tree songs.

D Write other poems as question and answer songs – 'Song of the waves', 'Song of the wind', 'Song of the mountains' and so on.

Copymaster 64 (Leaf shapes)

A Ask children to collect as many leaf words as possible, thinking of touch, colour, shape and sound (for dry leaves) and completing the lists on the copymaster. Short leaf poems (perhaps haiku) can then be written on leaf outlines traced from the copymaster. The leaves can be coloured, using faint coloured-pencil strokes, cut out and displayed on a 'branch'.

B Display tree poems on bark rubbings. Put them together to make an anthology of forest poems.

C Ask children to write poems about the different smells of trees – a spruce, trees after the rain, May blossom and so on.

D Imagine trees coming to life and marching through the forest. What would they think of busy roads, of seeing children in a playground, of a supermarket? Ask children to write a poem from the tree's point of view as it strides into town.

E Ask children to write a sequence poem in four quarters, describing one tree at each season of the year.

F Ask children to write the story of a Christmas tree, from being uprooted from the forest, to the warm living room where it is weighed down with decorations, to the day before Twelfth Night when it is put outdoors once again. The narrative poem should be full of wonder and sadness.

G Read 'November night' by Adelaide Crapsey below. This poem is a cinquain: 2–4–6–8–2 syllables in five lines.

Listen :
With faint dry sound,
Like steps of passing ghosts,
The leaves, frost-crisped, break from the trees
And fall.

Ask the children to write more cinquains on a forest theme. Display the poems on five-pointed leaves, one line for each point.

A tree has secrets

A tree has secrets,
Mystery tales in dark woods,
Silent, still and deep.

Andrew Mines

The silver tree

The silver tree hates the noisy forest:
the branches' grasp, the gossiping leaves;
the clack and caw of ragged birds,
the shadows deep as haunted screams.

She longs to cast her seeds so far
that they will grow in solitude:
alone in a city
surrounded by bright colours,
glowing lights, admiring eyes,
and the gentle hum of traffic.

Dave Ward

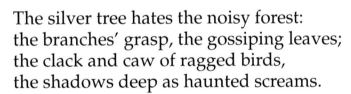

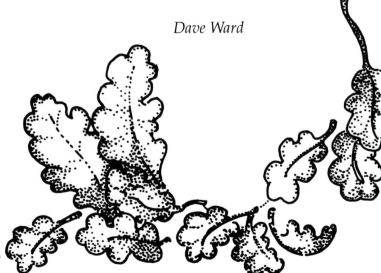

Imagine a world without trees

Never seeing _____

Never hearing _____

No home for _____

No place for _____

No _____

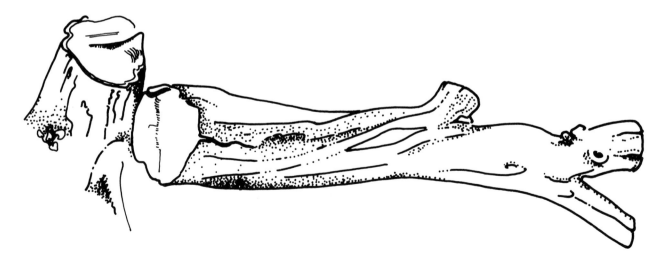

Write a sad chorus to go at the end of each verse. Display on a tree shape with a *No Entry* flap. Under the flap draw some of the things that would be lost in a world without trees.

Copymaster 61

Tree mini-poems

125

Copymaster 62

Tree songs

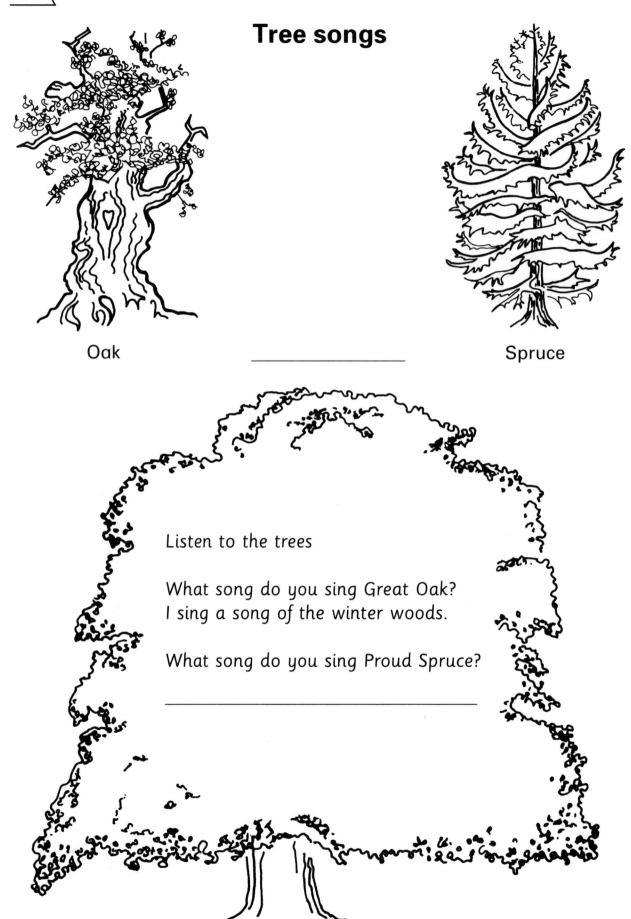

Oak   _____   Spruce

Listen to the trees

What song do you sing Great Oak?
I sing a song of the winter woods.

What song do you sing Proud Spruce?

_____

Write a question and answer poem for different trees. Use the poem for choral speaking and add a chorus for the whole forest.

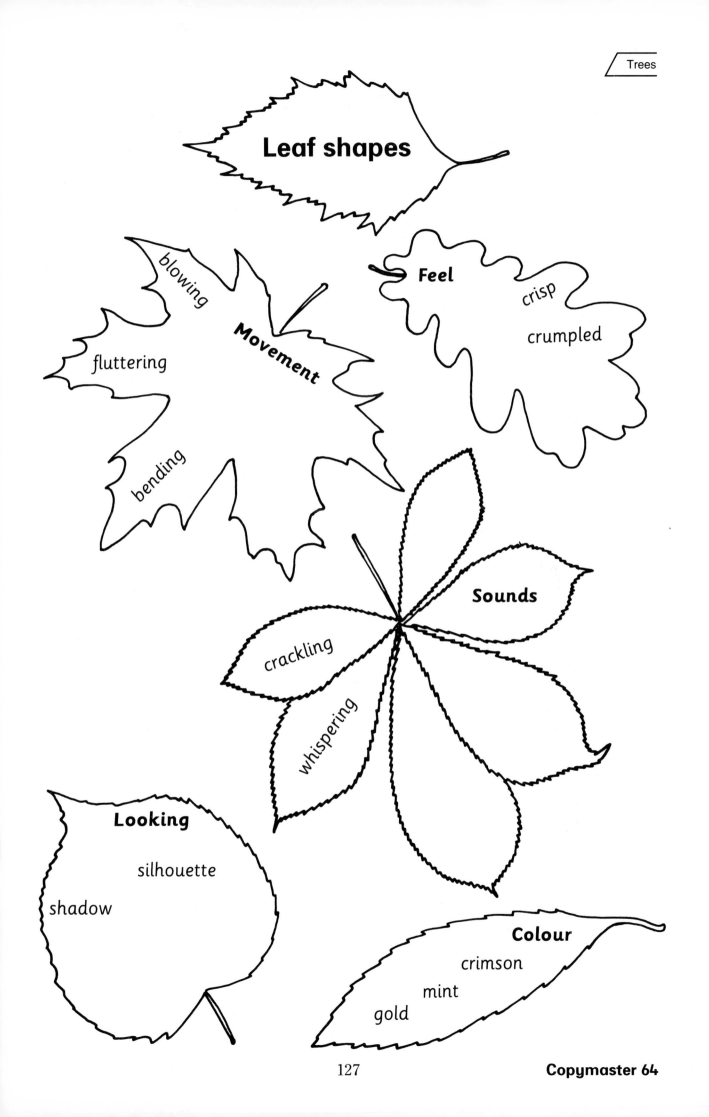

Leaf shapes

blowing

fluttering

Movement

bending

Feel

crisp

crumpled

Sounds

crackling

whispering

Looking

silhouette

shadow

Colour

crimson

mint

gold

127

Copymaster 64

WONDERFUL WORLD

The topic of environment is best handled in a positive way: better to suggest that 'It's a wonderful world – let's not spoil it!' rather than 'The world's in a mess – what can *we* do about it?' Children's poems about pollution and related environmental topics can very easily become no more than slogans, rather than thoughtful pieces of writing.

Copymaster 65 (Looking closely)

A This copymaster asks the children to combine scientific skills with those of the artist and poet. Suggest that they look outside for the smallest natural object they can find (certainly no bigger than something that can be held in the hand). This could be a daisy head, a fallen leaf or a pebble.

The children should look at the object like a scientist, noting where it was found, if changes have taken place in its structure and so on; like an artist, noting texture, shape and colour; like a poet, finding the best words to describe it and looking for unusual images.

Ask the children to draw the object and write notes. Using 'Looking closely' (in the Anthology, page 129) as a pattern, children should write a poem, asking a question in the first two lines, and answering it in no more than three lines.

B Make new rules for this kind of poem. Perhaps the children should not touch, as suggested, but just look.

C Bring a range of natural objects into the classroom – shells, pebbles, driftwood – and work in a similar way, using these as starters.

D Find a set of historical objects: war medals, a fan, a broken necklace, a pocket watch and so on. Encourage the children to examine each object closely, turning it over in their hands to find touch words, looking with a sense of wonder and thinking about the person who once owned and used these things. The question and answer format works well here, especially where the children are unsure of what some of the objects might have been used for, for example small kitchen or garden implements.

E Display the finished poems on a 'wall', each piece of writing in its own 'stone'.

Copymaster 66 (How to clean the world)

A Suggest that the children follow the pattern of writing a poem with two 'cleaning' ideas for each type of pollution problem. The first should be a somewhat outrageous idea, for example 'a force ten gale' to clear the world of air pollution, followed by a better solution, for example not to create the problem in the first place. There is a completed example of the type of poem wanted on the copymaster, followed by space to write more.

B Follow up by writing poems along the same lines for clearing up the school/street/village/town.

Copymaster 67 (Before and after)

A This copymaster gets its inspiration from advertisements that promise to change one's life or looks and often include before and after photographs. The children should first complete the river bank drawings, the bottom polluted the top unpolluted. They should then find descriptive words and ideas to write a poem of contrasts – A 'Wonderful world/terrible world' poem.

B Using the same outline idea, ask children to write a 'Now and then' poem about their town/village/street from old photographs. Children should first build up a suitable word bank, then work on a poem in two contrasting parts, 'Now' and 'Then'. This can fit in well with an historical theme on the local environment.

Copymaster 68 (Wonderful alphabet)

A In this activity it is not necessary to include every letter of the alphabet (although some children enjoy the challenge!). The letters are there as stimuli and the writer should aim at interesting and sensitive ideas rather than highly contrived ones. This task can be tackled by a group or as a class, with individual children being allocated or choosing particular letters. Every offering can be included in the final poem, or an editing session can select one idea (the most interesting, funniest, most unusual, etc.) for each letter.

B Display the finished poem, neatly printed or word-processed, as an alphabet book that can be presented to an infant class. The children can design an illustrated letter to begin each line, so that the book has the appeal of an illuminated manuscript.

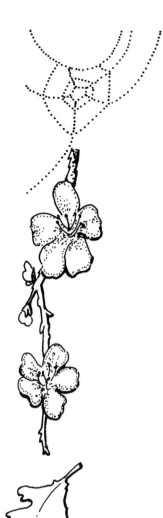

Fireweed in the park

The park keeper hates us:
We sneak out when he's not looking
And tell scarlet stories so shocking
That all the dusty old women
Start sneezing at once;
They trap the keeper in his hut,
Bang on the door with sticks,
Shout through his letter box
And threaten to do him a mischief;
So he rushes out in a rage
And chops and slashes and burns
And thinks he's done the trick.

What a laugh!
We've grown feathers,
Turned into a flock of doves,
And flown high over the fence.

Now we look for earth,
Earth as dark as a magician's hat.

David Orme

Looking closely

Kneel down and look –
a crystal ball, a moonstone?
No, just morning dew
hanging like a bauble
from a blade
of winter grass.

Reach up and touch –
a beaded net, a bridal veil?
No, just silver webs
draped like a shroud
over the bones
of skeleton trees.

Moira Andrew

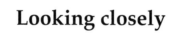

Looking closely

Read 'Looking closely'. Look closely at the smallest natural things *you* can find: a daisy, a fallen leaf, a cobweb. Don't touch, just look and draw.

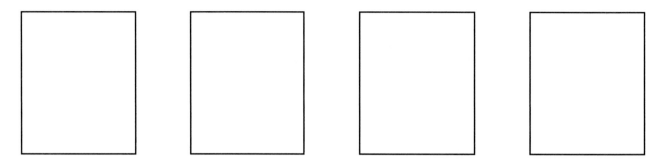

Begin your own poem, using 'Looking closely' as a pattern.
Look at the example below:

Kneel down and look –
a skeleton, a drifting boat?   (question)
No, just an autumn leaf   (answer)
    falling like a parachute
    from a bare-boned oak.

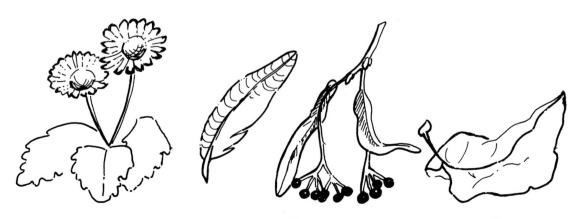

Copymaster 65

How to clean the world

Here are the cleaning instructions for the world. Unfortunately, most of the instructions have gone missing! Can you help?

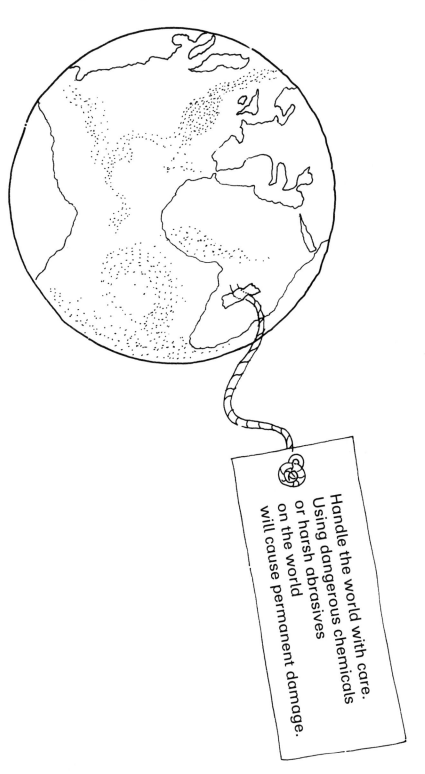

If the air is full of smoke
And car exhausts,
Bring up a force ten gale
To blow it out to sea.
Better still,
Try walking to school!

If

Handle the world with care.
Using dangerous chemicals
or harsh abrasives
on the world
will cause permanent damage.

Before and after

Look what has happened to the river! Write your 'Before and after' poem in the river. Remember, the polluted river might be the before, and the clean river after – if it has been cleaned up.

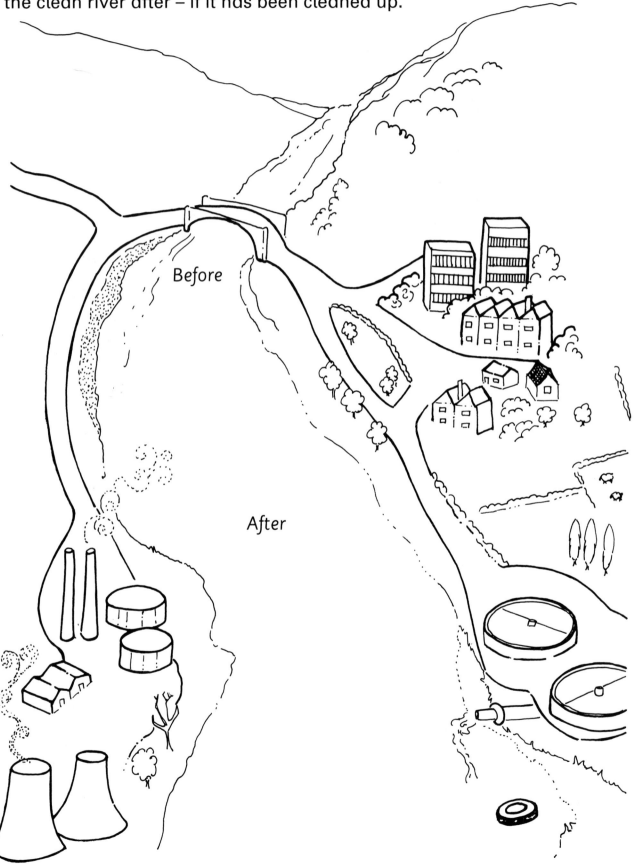

Before

After

Copymaster 67

Wonderful alphabet

The poet has given up on this poem! Can you help finish it off? What pattern does it have?

The wonderful alphabet world

Ants, rushing like people late for work,
Bluebells in a wood no-one has found,
Cold mornings with frost-leaves on the window,
Ditches, croaking with frogs,
Eggs in a hidden nest,
Flashes of lightning cracking the sky,
Green

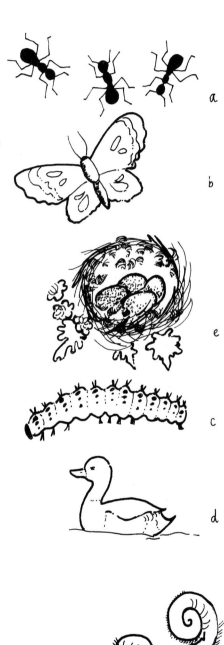

a

b

e

c

d

f

h

133   **Copymaster 68**

MACHINES

Children nowadays have grown up with machines and are often much more competent than adults at using them! This topic latches onto the children's interest and looks at machines from unusual points of view.

Copymaster 69 (Crazy machines)

A Before beginning work on this copymaster ask the children for way-out inventions – a machine to measure the distance from here to eternity, a machine to count the leaves on the tallest tree in the world, a machine to reach into space and so on.

Using the idea of a machine to paint the stars as an example, ask how the children might reach to the stars, for example by standing on top of the highest mountain in the world, using a ladder balancing on a pyramid, going on an escalator to take you to the top of a rainbow and so on. Go for really over-the-top suggestions which borrow from the natural world – rivers, mountains, rain clouds – then add things or creatures from the world of legend or from the imagination – giants, mermaids, hobbits.

Encourage the children to put these ideas together in lines in the style of a magical DIY manual, trying to keep some of the mystery of the original idea. Like the example shown on the copymaster, it will begin to sound and look like a poem.

B Ask children to draw each crazy machine and identify all the parts.

C Let children invent machines for more ordinary purposes: a machine to stop babies crying, a machine to weigh an elephant, a machine to airlift children to school and so on. Let one group suggest the idea and another invent the machine.

D Display the poems alongside the working drawings and invite parents to guess the purpose of each invention.

Copymaster 70 (Rackatack, rock and roll)

A This copymaster asks the children to listen to everyday mechanical sounds and to reproduce them, either in recognisable words or in a phonic representation. It should be a lot of fun – and may well be rather noisy!

Ask children to listen to the sound of a hair dryer, a vacuum cleaner or the caretaker's floor polisher and invent a rhythmic chant to represent it. Children should then put the sound-rhythms together with words to establish the machine's identity, for example 'a vacuum cleaner am I!' There is space for the children to write two chants, one for a washing machine and one for a machine of their own choice together with space for their own illustration.

B Ask children to listen to street sounds – the school bus, a motorbike revving up, a car accelerating from rest at the traffic lights to full speed on the motorway. Make up street 'music'.

C Work on the same idea for trains, aeroplanes and ferries, and make a set of transport songs.

D Both of the Anthology poems for this topic are about machine sounds. Develop this theme further with sound poems, using onomatopoeic words and percussion instruments. Use 'Listen to machines' as a model. Futuristic machines also make an interesting theme.

E Look for classroom and school machines, such as computers, pencil sharpeners and photocopiers. Ask children to write a poem in which the machine tells its story. 'Label' the machines with the children's poems.

F Add percussion to the rhythmic chants or mouth music and develop into a performance piece.

Copymaster 71 (Machines into animals)

A For this task the children have to be encouraged to think of the shape of the machine, the sounds it makes and its purpose, and find an idea for the most likely animal 'shadow': a train like a dragon, a digger like a dinosaur and so on.

B Now turn the idea on its head and ask children to look for a machine that is like an animal. What machine might a python resemble? A brown bear? A unicorn?

Copymaster 72 (I want to be human!)

A The first poem on the copymaster gives a machine its own personality: it suggests a sad robot. Ask children to complete the poem in the space on the copymaster and then try one about a friendly robot, an ambitious robot and a fierce robot. Each poem should begin:

If only I was human,
I could …

Encourage the children to try to get into the robot's skin, to think of all the things they can do that a robot can't. These should first be listed as ideas, then a rhythm found for them. Finally the ideas should be put together to make a list poem, full of feeling.

B The second poem on the copymaster suggests a child who wants to be a robot. To complete the poem children must think what they would like to be able to do, then why and then how.

C Use the same method for a poem called 'Invisible me', beginning:

If I were invisible,
I could …

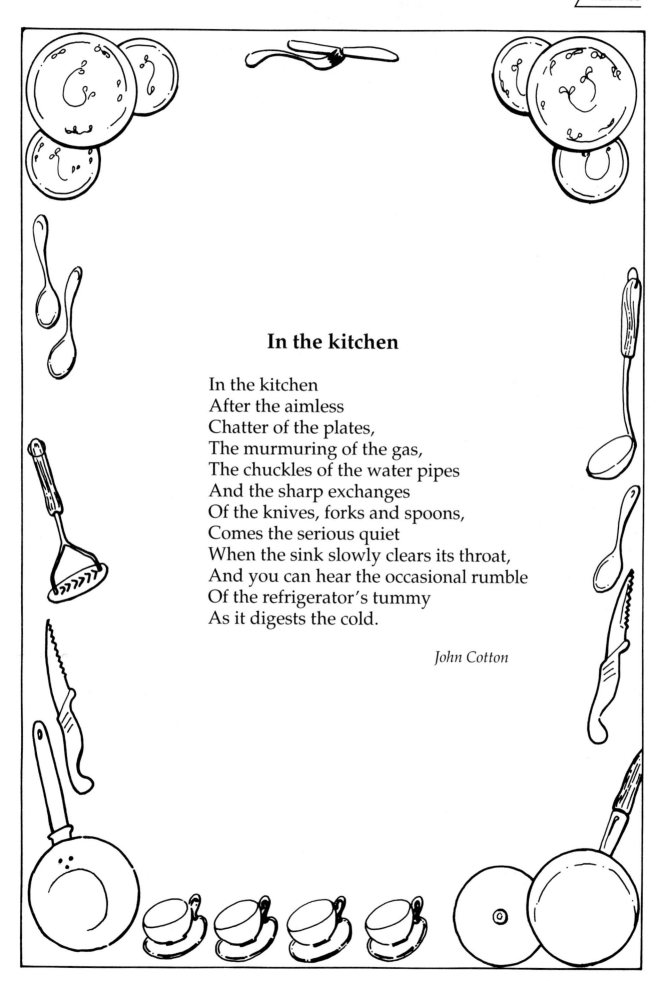

In the kitchen

In the kitchen
After the aimless
Chatter of the plates,
The murmuring of the gas,
The chuckles of the water pipes
And the sharp exchanges
Of the knives, forks and spoons,
Comes the serious quiet
When the sink slowly clears its throat,
And you can hear the occasional rumble
Of the refrigerator's tummy
As it digests the cold.

John Cotton

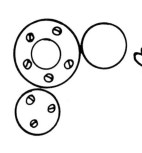

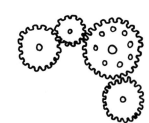

Listen to machines!

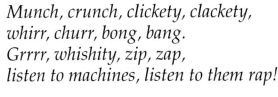

Munch, crunch, clickety, clackety,
whirr, churr, bong, bang.
Grrrr, whishity, zip, zap,
listen to machines, listen to them rap!

Machines, machines, machines, machines,
everywhere, everywhere, even in dreams.
Clanging, banging, whirring and gurring,
crashing, thrashing, cracking and whacking.
On roadways and railways,
on seaways and airways.
All we can hear are machines, machines,
the world is metal and plastic it seems.

Munch, crunch, clickety, clackety,
whirr, churr, bong, bang.
Grrrr, whishity, zip, zap,
listen to machines, listen to them rap!

Machine, machine, machine, machine,
everyone uses one even the Queen.
Washing, cooking, cleaning and preening,
digging, jigging, repairing and blaring.
Pumping, thumping, sprawling, stalling,
thunderous, blunderous, furious, curious.
Stereo, washing machine, car, bus
Soon there'll be no need for any of US!

Munch, crunch, clickety, clackety,
whirr, churr, bong, bang.
Grrrr, whishity, zip, zap,
listen to machines, listen to them rap!

Ian Souter

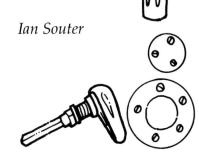

Crazy machines

Can you invent a crazy machine
to paint the stars?
Draw and write about it.

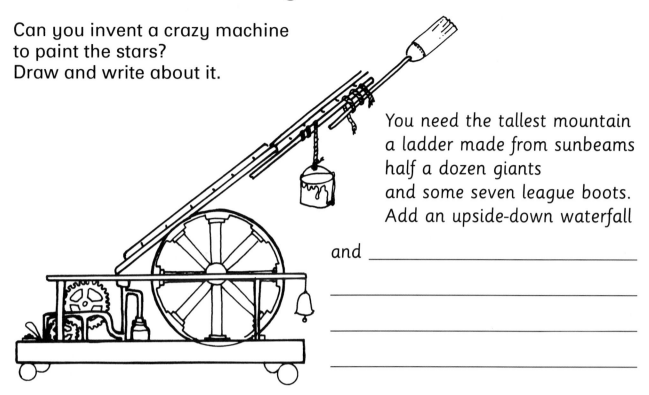

You need the tallest mountain
a ladder made from sunbeams
half a dozen giants
and some seven league boots.
Add an upside-down waterfall

and _____

_____

_____

_____

Can you invent a machine to count the grains of sand in the desert?

Invent your own crazy machine and ask your friends to guess its
purpose.

Copymaster 69

Rackatack, rock and roll

Listen to the rhythm of a machine. Think of words to describe it. Put them together to make mouth music.

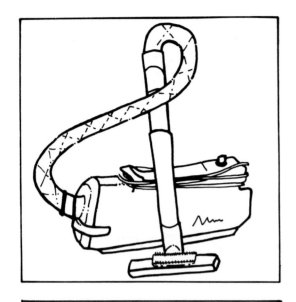

Brrm, brrm,
swoosh, whoosh
whizz, whizz, whizz
a vacuum cleaner
am I!

Copymaster 70

Machines into animals

Can you turn a machine into an animal?
The pictures might help, or you might
have a good idea of your own.

The train is a dragon

The train is a dragon.
It roars through the tunnel.
A ship roars back
through its funnel.

Jill Townsend

Write a poem following the pattern above.

The _____ is a _____

It _____

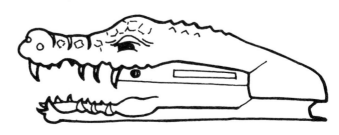

Copymaster 71

I want to be human!

Here is a robot that would like to be human; and someone who would like to be a robot!

Can you finish their poems?

If only I was human,
I could

If only I was a robot,
I could

Copymaster 72